...ing Edge series

...ditor

...n with *MIT Sloan Management Review*

...ed Koenigsberg, *The Ends Game: How Smart Companies Stop ...art Delivering Value*

...lia Hautz, Kurt Matzler, and Stephan Friedrich von den Eichen, *...ring Disruption from Outside the C-Suite*

...Nanda, Anh Nguyen Phillips, and Jonathan Copulsky, *The ...th: Leading Your Organization through Uncertain Times*

...ing the Right Game: How to Disrupt, Defend, and Deliver in a

...n and Yadong Luo, *The Digital Multinational: Navigating the New ...al Business*

...san and John W. Boudreau, *Work without Jobs: How to Reboot Your ...s Work Operating System*

...ramaniam, *The Future of Competitive Strategy: Unleashing the Power of Data ...Ecosystems*

...ngham and Rory M. McDonald, *Productive Tensions: How Every Leader Can ...ovation's Toughest Trade-Offs*

...H. Davenport and Steven M. Miller, *Working with AI: Real Stories of Human– ...Collaboration*

...rathy, *Enterprise Strategy for Blockchain: Lessons in Disruption from Fintech, ...Chains, and Consumer Industries*

...a Gratton, *Redesigning Work: How to Transform Your Organization and Make ...id Work for Everyone*

...n Horn, *Inside the Competitor's Mindset: How to Predict Their Next Move and ...ition Yourself for Success*

...izabeth J. Altman, David Kiron, Jeff Schwartz, and Robin Jones, *Workforce ...cosystems: Reaching Strategic Goals with People, Partners, and Technologies*

Barbara H. Wixom, Cynthia M. Beath, and Leslie Owens, *Data Is Everybody's Business: The Fundamentals of Data Monetization*

Eric Siegel, *The AI Playbook: Mastering the Rare Art of Machine Learning Deployment*

Malia C. Lazu, *From Intention to Impact: A Practical Guide to Diversity, Equity, and Inclusion*

Daniel Aronson, *The Value of Values: How Leaders Can Grow Their Businesses and Enhance Their Careers by Doing the Right Thing*

Benjamin Laker, Lebene Soga, Yemisi Bolade-Ogunfodun, and Adeyinka Adewale, *Job Crafting*

Andreas von der Gathen, Nicolai Broby Eckert, and Caroline Kastbjerg, *The Demand Revolution: How Consumers Are Redefining Sustainability and Transforming the Future of Business*

MITSloan
Management Review

T0245932

The D...

Revolu...

...on the Cut...

...erg, series e...

...cooperati...

...ni and Oc...
...ucts and S...
...tadler, Ju...
...egy: Mast...
...ne, Rich...
...ation M...
...er, Win...
...World...
...ambisa...
...n Glob...
...sutha...
...ation...
...Sub...
...B. B...
...Inn...
...has...
...ing...
...Sa...
...ly...
...d...
...in...

The Demand Revolution

How Consumers Are Redefining Sustainability
and Transforming the Future of Business

Andreas von der Gathen, Nicolai Broby Eckert, and
Caroline Kastbjerg

The MIT Press
Cambridge, Massachusetts
London, England

© 2024 Massachusetts Institute of Technology

All rights reserved. No part of this book may be used to train artificial intelligence systems or reproduced in any form by any electronic or mechanical means (including photocopying, recording, or information storage and retrieval) without permission in writing from the publisher.

The MIT Press would like to thank the anonymous peer reviewers who provided comments on drafts of this book. The generous work of academic experts is essential for establishing the authority and quality of our publications. We acknowledge with gratitude the contributions of these otherwise uncredited readers.

This book was set in ITC Stone Serif Std and ITC Stone Sans Std by New Best-set Typesetters Ltd. Printed and bound in the United States of America.

Library of Congress Cataloging-in-Publication Data

Names: Gathen, Andreas von der, author. | Eckert, Nicolai Broby, author. | Kastbjerg, Caroline, author.
Title: The demand revolution : how consumers are redefining sustainability and transforming the future of business / Andreas von der Gathen, Nicolai Broby Eckert, and Caroline Kastbjerg.
Description: Cambridge, Massachusetts : The MIT Press, [2024] | Series: Management on the cutting edge | Includes bibliographical references and index.
Identifiers: LCCN 2023057583 (print) | LCCN 2023057584 (ebook) | ISBN 9780262049320 (hardcover) | ISBN 9780262380218 (epub) | ISBN 9780262380201 (pdf)
Subjects: LCSH: Sustainable development. | Consumption (Economics)—Environmental aspects. | Value.
Classification: LCC HC79.E5 G345 2024 (print) | LCC HC79.E5 (ebook) | DDC 338.9/27—dc23/eng/20231214
LC record available at https://lccn.loc.gov/2023057583
LC ebook record available at https://lccn.loc.gov/2023057584

10 9 8 7 6 5 4 3 2 1

To our family, friends, and colleagues and our shared hope for a more sustainable future

Contents

Series Foreword

The world does not lack for management ideas. Thousands of researchers, practitioners, and other experts produce tens of thousands of articles, books, papers, posts, and podcasts each year. But only a scant few promise to truly move the needle on practice, and fewer still dare to reach into the future of what management will become. It is this rare breed of idea—meaningful to practice, grounded in evidence, and *built for the future*—that we seek to present in this series.

Abbie Lundberg

Editor in chief

MIT Sloan Management Review

Preface

The more exposure we had to sustainability in our work over the past decade, the more curious we became to understand why so many investments in sustainability do not seem to pay off as expected. The tipping point came in 2018 after a meeting with a CEO who told us a story that we have heard many times, before and since. It inspired us to start working on a book, but we had no idea at the time that it would evolve into the book you now have in your hands.

The CEO wanted advice on how to build a successful sustainability strategy or, more specifically, how to commercialize the investments his company had made. Its extensive market research showed that consumers have a desire for green products and willingness to pay for them, but when it launched its first sustainable offering, that offering fell far short of expectations.

It was clear that many other leaders were also struggling to make the business case for investments in sustainable solutions. They poured significant sums into sustainable product lines or into reducing their carbon dioxide footprint, but the financial upside remained elusive. That led them to slow down their pace of investment in sustainability and to view it as a compliance obligation instead of as a lever for strategic growth.

Consumers, meanwhile, were telling a different story. Our extensive market and pricing research clearly showed that sustainability was rapidly becoming a value driver and purchasing criterion for consumers across more and more product categories. So why was there a disconnect between these findings and the financial performance of companies? Were consumers exaggerating? Were companies missing something?

We initially thought about writing a book about how to monetize sustainability. But as our research continued, we recognized that the underlying issues of commercializing sustainability went far beyond prices and willingness to pay. We started to explore four questions:

- Why do so many companies fail in their sustainability efforts?
- What makes sustainability different from other consumer trends or megatrends?
- What do consumers *really* think about sustainability, and what does this mean for companies trying to win them over?
- How can companies use those consumer insights to create successful sustainability strategies?

The story seemed doomed to have the same ending, with dashed hopes and unfulfilled expectations. Then we started to listen more closely to what consumers were telling us. Their insights became the source of our answers to all four questions and the basis for this book. It is our humble hope that *The Demand Revolution* will give you and other business leaders a clearer and stronger foundation for strategic decisions about sustainability and that it will inspire you to make bold moves.

I The Fatal Disconnect: Why Companies Fail to See the Market Opportunity from Sustainability

1 Sustainability—as We Know It—Is Not Sustainable

Is Amazon a failed business?

That may seem like an odd question for the beginning of a book about consumers and sustainability. But Amazon's evolution over the past 30 years exposes some of the fatal disconnects in how companies are approaching sustainability from a business perspective. The effect of Amazon on people's day-to-day lives has become so pervasive that it is easy to forget that company's original success came from selling books online, at a discount, out of a garage in Seattle, Washington.[1] In the article "The Next Big Thing: A Bookstore?" in 1996, *Fortune* interviewed Amazon founder Jeff Bezos, who cited two simple keys to success: "comprehensive selection ('Our goal is that if it's in print, it's in stock') and 10% to 30% discounts on most books."[2]

A snapshot of the company's first website, included in that *Fortune* article, underscores that value proposition. The company, then privately held and known as Amazon.com, offered "one million titles [and] consistently low prices" and told visitors that "if you explore just one thing, make it our personal notification service. We think it's very cool!" The Amazon logo included the tagline "Earth's biggest bookstore." Bezos explained why he chose this discount-driven strategy. "It's a huge mistake not to offer discounts," he said. "Most online businesses fail because they mis-estimate the value proposition."[3]

Fast-forward almost a couple of decades, and consumers are keenly aware of how the Amazon story turned out. The marketing data and analytics firm Kantar ranks Amazon as the world's fourth most valuable brand, trailing only Apple, Microsoft, and Google.[4] Amazon described the Prime Day it held on July 11, 2023, as "the single largest sales day in company history. Over the course of the two-day shopping event, Prime members purchased more than 375 million items worldwide and saved more than $2.5 billion on millions of deals across the Amazon store, helping make it the biggest Prime Day event ever."[5] Investors also know how the Amazon story turned out. At the end of September 2023, the company's market capitalization stood at $1.29 trillion.[6]

Now imagine that Amazon had made the "huge mistake" that Bezos mentioned and had eschewed discounts in favor of a different strategy. Let's assume that Amazon established its businesses with the belief that an investment makes sense only if the company can extract a premium price from consumers. This is not far-fetched. Ordering a book from one's computer and having it appear on the doorstep a few days later is a value proposition that offers consumers—at least in theory—a much greater utility because of the improved convenience. Why shouldn't Amazon therefore adopt a premium strategy to claim a share of that added value? Why shouldn't consumers pay that premium to help Amazon offset the immense costs required to establish an online bookstore in the early days of the internet, never mind keep it running and subsidize its growth?

If Bezos had followed that philosophy, Amazon and its early investors would have considered the business a failure unless they succeeded in charging more—not less—for printed books. They certainly would not have endured 20 years of losses or minimal profits since Amazon's founding in 1994.[7]

Amazon and its investors would have also taken their logic one step further. They would have concluded that if consumers did not want to pay a premium for convenience, then the theory about the greater utility of convenience must be false. In that case, why should Amazon invest heavily in an easy-to-use and intuitive interface with bells and whistles such as personal notification and, later, the ability for consumers to write and publish their own reviews? In the absence of a consumer commitment to pay a premium price, such investments would be profit-killing dead ends.

But Amazon did not follow that path. Rather than operate as if "premium" were the only viable strategy and price position, Bezos and his company committed themselves to ensuring that consumers not only paid *less* for books and other products but also enjoyed an easy way to make those less expensive purchases. By doing so, it disproved two hypotheses about the launch of a product or service, especially one with the potential to reach a massive scale: first, consumers' willingness to pay a premium price is essential to success, and, second, consumers' unwillingness to pay a premium indicates their rejection of the merits of that product or service.

These two hypotheses have unfortunately guided the prevailing thinking about sustainable products and services.[8] Business leaders widely assume that consumers must pay more for sustainable solutions and that they are uninterested in sustainability if they do not pay more. These assumptions permeate management thinking to such an extent that even the business media reflexively seeks the existence of a premium when it reports on a company's attempts to take its ostensibly sustainable solutions to market.

When the *Wall Street Journal* ran a feature story in 2022 about a disposable razor that the US personal-care products company Schick had designed to "appeal to environmentally conscious consumers," it highlighted a potential appeal that could anchor the razor's value proposition. It quoted the sustainability director of an advertising agency as saying that "evidencing responsibly sourced materials, reducing the amount of packaging, and removing toxic or environmentally damaging ingredients are high on the list for today's educated consumer." Then in the next paragraph, the article noted that "there are challenges for marketers, including determining *whether and when consumers will bear any extra costs*." It cited a study on consumers and sustainability that claimed that "66% said they are not willing to pay more for sustainable products or services."[9]

Taking the presumed absence of a price premium as a rejection of a value proposition is a fatal disconnect that contributes to what we call the *green mirage*. It expresses the logic—repeated ad nauseum in the business press and in boardrooms around the world—about why sustainability is bad business. For decades, so the story goes, consumers have been unwilling to pay premium prices to offset the immense costs of developing sustainable offerings and bringing them to market. Criticisms and indictments of research into sustainability and consumer behavior often call out this yawning gap between intentions and actions.

This thinking has provided ample ammunition for the critics of sustainable business, who argue that consumers consistently refuse to put their money where their mouth is. They place the blame squarely on consumers, in the spirit of a statement usually attributed to the anthropologist Margaret Mead: "What people say, what people do, and what they say they do are entirely different things."[10]

The Fatal Disconnects of the Green Mirage

Instead of pursuing innovative applications or developing irresistible sustainable products or services, companies that buy into the green mirage confine themselves to solutions that are either more expensive or lower-quality versions of things consumers already buy and generally like. They compromise by making small investments in sustainability that may enhance their reputation or help them fulfill environmental, societal, and governance (ESG) commitments. Without the promise of a price premium, they believe, anything beyond those niche or token efforts is doomed to be unprofitable and therefore not worth pursuing. In other words, they follow the exact opposite of the strategy that made Amazon successful.

Let's take a deeper look at the fatal disconnects of the green mirage. The first disconnect is that consumers' lack of willingness to pay more for currently available sustainable solutions is proof that they have no interest in sustainability. This assumption equates "paying more" with "caring," and the absence of the former negates the latter. The green mirage blames consumers for the apparently fizzled waves of sustainable initiatives because they haven't opened their wallets to pay the bill for a sustainable transformation.

The second fatal disconnect rests on the assumption that if consumers are not willing to pay more, then they must be willing to make sacrifices on sustainable product attributes or on customer experience and thus to accept inferior products. We refer to this disconnect as the *quality penalty*. It leads companies to focus on how much consumers are willing to sacrifice, not on the benefits they will derive from a solution. It means asking consumers to subjugate or forsake their other individual needs—such as convenience, affordability, safety, health, or performance—rather than satisfy them. As our extensive research shows in part III, consumers are well aware of this quality penalty. They tend to perceive existing sustainable solutions as hard to find, of inferior or parity quality, exorbitantly priced, and backed by dubious claims.

The ideas that consumers need to pay either a premium price or a quality penalty to cover a company's higher costs have become illusory truths, repeated so often and so widely that businesspeople take them for granted.[11] Yet at the same time companies are often guilty of the same duplicity they accuse consumers of practicing. In one study, 63 percent of industry professionals reported that their company was prioritizing ESG issues when making business decisions. However, only 14 percent were currently publishing ESG-specific reports.[12] A report by the World Economic Forum stated that 90 percent of executives believe sustainability is important, but only 60 percent of organizations have sustainability strategies.[13]

The illusory truths also influence how companies define and frame the challenges in creating sustainability strategies. They frequently frame the challenges as conflicts expressed in easily digestible terms, such as "doing good versus making money" and "purpose versus profit." The purpose claim is that every person and every business ought to have a purpose aimed at saving the planet or at least achieving specific ESG objectives. The profit claim is that none of these grand purposes will be sustainable—in terms of being both enduring and environmentally sound—unless businesses can earn a profit. The persistent inability to resolve these conflicts turns the pursuit of scalable, profitable sustainable solutions into a fool's errand, making it easy, perhaps inevitable, for companies to accept unprofitable business cases—derived from the assumptions of the green mirage—as justification to postpone, slow down, or kill sustainable initiatives.

We agree that no one can force a company to pursue a profit opportunity that doesn't exist, no matter how strong, overwhelming, emotional, or purposeful the rhetoric is. Businesses can't save the world if consumers in their markets don't want to be saved or are unwilling to take an active role. But we disagree with the assumptions underlying the green mirage. Its fatal disconnects are making sustainability—as we know it—unsustainable. We contend that a vast common ground exists for businesses and consumers in the marketplace. In this book, we show how the past 60 years of awareness and exposure to sustainability have reshaped consumer behavior, reset their expectations, and made a majority of consumers willing to buy sustainable solutions, assuming those solutions offer the right combination of affordability, accessibility, quality, and trustworthy messaging.

That's why we don't frame the problem of sustainable business using the simplistic dichotomies of "doing good versus making money" and "purpose versus profit." Nor do we frame the marketplace as an oversimplified, binary battle between "green" solutions and "gray" solutions, with the latter so named because their value depends heavily on the use of fossil fuels. Instead, we frame the future of sustainability through the lens of what we call a demand revolution.[14]

A *demand revolution* occurs when irresistible consumer pull at scale becomes the disruptive driving force that leads to the creation of new markets, new products, new ecosystems, and exponential growth.

Sustainability can be the next transformative megatrend on par with previous ones such as digitalization, globalization, mass production, and electrification. Whether that happens will come down to the choices companies make. How many will continue to subscribe to the flawed assumptions and fatal disconnects of the green mirage, and how many will embrace and capitalize on the demand revolution?

The Green Mirage versus the Demand Revolution

Refuting the assumptions of the green mirage must start with a brief look at how pricing strategies work, what factors drive profit, and how consumer behavior is changing.

The green mirage implies that the only practical commercial strategy for sustainability—out of all feasible strategies and price positions—is a skimming strategy with a premium-price position. But why should the success of a strategy depend solely on whether consumers *pay* more (price versus cost) and not, for example, on whether they *buy* more? Companies should expect consumers to pay a premium only if they serve consumer needs with better products, not just try to sell them ostensibly green ones.

The focus on skimming with a premium-price position obscures the fact that companies have other pricing strategies (e.g., penetration) and other price positions to choose from. In their book *Price Management: Strategy, Analysis, Decision, Implementation*, Hermann Simon and Martin Fassnacht break down these options for price positions into five categories: luxury, premium, medium, low, and ultralow.[15] In other words, companies can take many paths to become extraordinarily successful without the rigid and inflexible belief that every product needs a premium price, the same belief that is handicapping efforts to commercialize sustainable products. Amazon, much to the delight of its investors and customers, did not confine its choices to a premium-price strategy. Implementing a low-price strategy fueled Amazon's ability to scale its model into a massive global e-commerce business whose "size, scale, and cultural influence has driven several other key megatrends besides online shopping[,] including electric vehicles, e-commerce real estate, and cloud computing."[16]

The myopic focus on premium strategies also limits how companies assess profit opportunities. When companies invest in sustainable technologies and try to make the transition away from legacy processes, their prevailing presumption is that they can't earn a profit unless they can pass on those costs to customers in the form of higher prices. The basic equation for profit, however, includes three variables, not two: profit is also a function of volume.[17]

The green mirage strips volume out of the equation and thus reduces the profit calculus to price and cost. High costs imply the need for a premium strategy, but that holds true only if one looks solely at current costs and potential prices in isolation. Doing that neglects the entire discussion of whether a consumer's purchase volume, purchase frequency, and loyalty also play a role. In other words, consumers' future decision-making doesn't enter the picture, nor does the potential for lower costs of solutions at scale. These limited calculations based on price and cost also fail to account for behavioral effects, such as the power that prices have at thresholds, in relation to each other, and in other contexts. Prices influence buying behavior beyond the ways that a rational buyer or seller who views a price in isolation would expect.

We are not ignoring that the costs of sustainable business can be significantly higher than prices in the short term as companies invest in capacity and develop new technologies to help them scale. The performance of Ford Motor Company with its electric vehicles (EVs) in 2023 highlights how both a short-term and a long-term perspective can skew the relationship among price, cost, and volume. Ford lost an estimated $36,000 on each EV it delivered to dealers in the third quarter of 2023. But the company's CFO, John Lawler, put that current gap between price and cost into perspective. "Startups lose money as they invest in capability, develop knowledge, build volume and gain share," he said at a media briefing. He also noted that "great product is not enough in the EV business anymore. We have to be totally competitive on cost." In his view, Tesla has set a "high benchmark for rivals by trimming cost and scaling output."[18]

We believe that profitable sustainable solutions require volume. They require companies to achieve scale quickly and harvest its advantages. They also require companies to stop looking at current snapshots of price and cost and start taking scale effects, such as the experience curve, into their calculations. This will help them make sustainable solutions more affordable over time.

The affordability of sustainable solutions is crucial for several reasons. One is that most consumers cannot afford the full "premiumization" of their daily lives as they try to live more sustainably. Perhaps most importantly, affordability is one of the major barriers to adoption for almost all consumers who are seeking sustainable solutions. Affordability is linked to a consumer's ability to pay and not just to their willingness to pay. Consumers with limited resources or tight budgets may have a legitimate willingness to pay for a particular product or service, but they forgo a purchase because the trade-offs they must make to meet their day-to-day needs leave them without an ability to pay.

In short, the green mirage imposes artificial constraints that make it almost impossible for a company to build a long-term, lucrative business case for investing in sustainable solutions. Removing those constraints starts with deeper understanding not only of what consumers want, need, and are willing to pay for but also of what motivates them, what barriers they face, and how they make their purchase decisions.

The existence of a consumer segmentation based on sustainability shows how consumer behavior is changing and marks a fundamental difference between the demand revolution and the green mirage. The green mirage reduces sustainable consumers to two broad segments: those willing to pay a premium for any given solution and those who won't. It assumes that the former group thus cares about sustainability, whereas the latter group does not because it is unwilling or unable to pay a premium for it. Furthermore, it assumes that the former segment is small—to the extent that it exists at all—while the latter segment represents most consumers. That is a gross caricature of how sustainability is influencing consumer behavior. It ignores the fact that sustainability has been in the public consciousness since the 1960s. The ensuing six decades of conditioning have reset how consumers think and have yielded a well-structured and stratified consumer segmentation that we sketch here briefly and describe in detail in part III.

The demand revolution builds on the idea that there is no such thing as a "sustainable consumer." Instead, consumers fall into several segments or archetypes based on their interest, commitment, actions, and willingness to pay for sustainable solutions. The segmentation we detail in part III is made up of eight archetypes of consumers along a spectrum from champions to nonbelievers. The champions make sustainability a driving force behind all their purchasing decisions. They rank it as a top purchase driver in almost every category and are willing to pay a premium for sustainable solutions. But they comprise only 8 percent of consumers. The nonbelievers, meanwhile, never view sustainability as a purchase criterion and are not willing to pay a premium for any such solutions. They account for 15 percent of the consumer population.

The champions and nonbelievers correspond to the two broad segments implied by the green mirage. But instead of considering those two segments as the entire market, the demand revolution focuses on the 77 percent of the population that lies between those two extremes. These consumers—who constitute the other six archetypes—have at least some interest and desire to purchase sustainable goods and services. The commercial opportunities for sustainable solutions therefore come not from a small sliver of consumers at one end of the consumer spectrum but rather from the 85 percent of the population, represented not only by the champions (8 percent) but also by six other archetypes (77 percent).

The percentages here come from surveys that Simon-Kucher conducted in 2021–2022. The surveys included respondents from 19 countries around the world, but unless otherwise stated, the data and insights we report in this book derive only from the respondents in Europe and North America. The vast majority of the European and North American respondents ranked sustainability among their top-five purchasing criteria in one or more product categories. This means that sustainability has joined traditional purchase criteria—price, quality, and brand—as a fundamental driver behind purchase decisions rather than as a fringe or niche one that influences only a small number of passionate consumers. As a result, some 34 percent of European and American respondents said they have made significant changes in their purchasing behavior or have even turned around their way of living over the past five years to be environmentally sustainable. Furthermore, 56 percent of consumers found environmental sustainability more important when making day-to-day purchase decisions than they did the previous year.[19] "Although customers are still price-conscious in their everyday shopping, a shift in value drivers can be observed," said Marit van Egmond, the CEO of Albert Heijn, the largest supermarket chain in the Netherlands. She added, "In addition to quality, taste and shelf life, sustainability is becoming increasingly important. This is increasingly reflected on today's shelves in all the different product ranges."[20]

These consumers are also doing their own research into sustainable solutions. If they don't find something that meets their needs, they find proxies for sustainability, such as quality, durability, and longevity. They define sustainability in personal terms and do not view sustainability as a yes–no feature. They instead look at the extent of how sustainable features and benefits contribute to the overall value of a solution.

The Imperatives of the Demand Revolution

Whether sustainability will be the greatest commercial opportunity of the twenty-first century depends on how quickly companies recognize consumer needs—both hidden and overt—and develop affordable, practical, and environmentally viable solutions to meet those needs. When business leaders see the green mirage's flawed logic and look beyond it, they become open to embracing the four imperatives that will help them capitalize on consumers' pent-up demand and the behavioral shifts that are generating it.

Put the Consumer First

This seems like an obvious recommendation from a business book, but the green mirage presents a unique situation. One of the green mirage's insidious and enduring effects is that it imposes arbitrary and unjustified constraints on business leaders who want to make a difference, and it biases the investors whose capital they need. By prescribing that companies should stereotype consumers instead of listening to their needs and serving them, the green mirage takes a blow torch to the idea of customer centricity, one of the bedrocks of marketing strategy in the twenty-first century.

Putting the consumer first means understanding what solutions and experiences they want and need—across the entire spectrum of consumer archetypes—rather than simply asking, "How much more will they pay for that thing I claim is green?" A customer-centric approach has its roots in the research and insights of marketing pioneers such as Peter Drucker and Theodore Levitt, who insisted that the success of any commercial undertaking starts and ends with meeting the needs of customers. As Drucker states in *The Practice of Management*, "What the business thinks it produces is not of first importance—especially not to the future of the business and to its success. What the customer thinks he is buying, what he considers 'value,' is decisive—it determines what a business is, what it produces and whether it will prosper." For that reason, Drucker contends that "any business enterprise has two—and only these two—basic functions: marketing and innovation."[21]

When writing about the success of industrial-goods companies in his book *Marketing Myopia*, Levitt points out that "without a very sophisticated eye on the customer, most of their new products might have been wrong, their sales methods useless." He expressed a similar thought in his article under the same title in *Harvard Business Review* in 1975: "The view that an industry is a customer-satisfying process, not a goods-producing process, is vital for all businesspeople to understand. An industry begins with the customer and his or her needs, not with a patent, a raw material, or a selling skill. Given the customer's needs, the industry develops backwards, first concerning itself with the physical delivery of customer satisfactions. Then it moves back further to creating the things by which these satisfactions are in part achieved."[22] Amazon embodies that philosophy as well, as expressed in the book *Working Backwards*, coauthored by former Amazon senior leaders Colin Bryan and Bill Carr. It describes the "product development process that gives this book its name: working backwards from the desired customer experience."[23]

Companies that ignore consumers will by default overemphasize the supply side of their business. They risk placing an undue emphasis on their technological, logistical, manufacturing, and process capabilities. In other words, they dismiss the "pull" side and build their business around the "push" side. We agree that eliminating waste, implementing environmentally sound processes throughout the value chain, and reducing carbon emissions are essential to securing the health of the planet for future generations. Nevertheless, companies that follow the imperatives of the demand revolution will also strive for an integration of the push and pull sides. These sides should be codependent, not separate. That point leads to the next imperative.

Change the Innovation Paradigm

Companies will not be able to unlock the pent-up demand in the markets—even if they recognize it—by sticking with old paradigms for innovation, which call for conventional go-to-market strategies and come with expectations of high initial premiums and slow adoption.

The traditional innovation paradigm takes a product idea through several adoption phases. It starts with early adopters who pay premium prices and help finance additional growth, then it ends with laggards who buy the product at a lower price at a time when it has reached an advanced stage in its technological life cycle or has seen its advantages eroded by competition.

For several reasons, the demand revolution warrants a new paradigm for innovation. This new paradigm encompasses a company's entire business model and extended ecosystem, while placing consumers at the core of future product innovations. Speed, in terms of time to market, matters far more than ever, because of the pent-up consumer demand for sustainable solutions that already exists in most markets. Companies that move first by offering such solutions will experience near instant uptake in adoption as long as their solutions remain aligned with consumer needs and preferences and stay within consumers' affordability thresholds. This pent-up demand also creates commercial opportunities for companies to achieve lasting first-mover advantages built on consumer loyalty and upselling opportunities.

The ability to accelerate adoption also matters because most markets for sustainable solutions will not have sufficient price premiums to allow the traditional adoption patterns to unfold. These markets will call for penetration strategies instead of skimming strategies and will also require other price positions besides premium. Companies too often take a technological or "push" approach to innovation rather than a "pull" one that helps them design products to meet customer needs or to hit target prices based on consumers' actual willingness to pay.

Speed and acceleration are harder to achieve when a company places too much emphasis on the supply side and on internally focused improvements. An article in the *MIT Sloan Management Review* advocated in 1999 that "managers should seek to reduce the 'ecological footprint' of their firms' activities by reinventing products and processes." It also called sustainable development "one of the biggest opportunities in the history of commerce."[24] Supply-side changes obviously take a long time to unfold, despite their promise. They also run the risk of focusing too much on the product itself and too little on the consumer.

The new paradigm for innovation must therefore be a combination of relentless consumer focus and the necessary capabilities to develop innovative sustainable solutions and take them to market. We contend that the classic adoption curves for innovations—and the strategic playbooks derived from those insights—no longer apply. Those innovation paradigms are neither fast enough nor able to confer a traditional second-mover advantage.

Change the Go-to-Market Strategy

Once freed from the confinements of a skimming strategy that requires a premium-price position or a quality penalty, business leaders have a wide range of options to take their consumer-driven innovations to market. We group these options into two broad categories—commercial creativity and creative destruction—and devote part IV to showing companies how to apply them.

Commercial creativity covers the ability to innovate business models quickly and effectively to bring successful sustainable solutions to market. Broadly speaking, it encompasses a company's willingness and ability to reengineer every cylinder of its revenue engine in response to consumer demand.[25] The creativity comes in as a company seeks to break away from traditional approaches as it breaks down consumers' barriers of affordability, accessibility, knowledge, and trust. Creative destruction, as defined by Joseph Schumpeter, refers to the "process of industrial mutation that continuously revolutionizes the economic structure from within, incessantly destroying the old one, incessantly creating a new one."[26]

Tesla's success shows how commercial creativity and creative destruction go hand in hand and how that success—to borrow the phrase from Ford CFO John Lawler—sets a high benchmark for incumbent original equipment manufacturers (OEMs) in the EV market. Tesla did more than bring a zero-emission EV to market. It launched a better vehicle powered by electricity and supported by the company's own ecosystem in terms of sales, service, and charging stations. The company also has the long-term objective of offering EVs at affordable prices.

This marketing strategy not only emphasizes product benefits but also directly addresses consumers concerns about affordability, accessibility, knowledge, and trust. Tesla has no dealer network and does not depend on aftermarket sales and service for revenue in the ways that incumbent OEMs do. Ford CEO Jim Farley has estimated that this marketing approach gives Tesla "a cost advantage of $2,000 a car."[27] Until 2023, Tesla had also never invested in traditional advertising, in contrast to the incumbent OEMs, who spend billions of dollars per year on ads. The company has instead relied on social media, consumer advocacy, and the media presence of CEO Elon Musk.[28] These new approaches leave incumbents with their own challenges in terms of commercial creativity and creative destruction as they try to adapt their existing business models, ecosystems, and interactions with consumers.

Communicate Clearly

This seems like another obvious recommendation, but once again the green mirage presents a unique situation. Communication about sustainability has more often been a disabler than an enabler, depending on what companies choose to say about their actions and intentions.

Communication's role as a disabler comes in many forms, from fear mongering and doomsday scenarios to greenwashing in explicit or implicit forms. Even the word *green* and its use as a prefix (in, e.g., *greenwashing, greenhushing, greenfluencing*) or as a universal modifier undermines communication because it emphasizes a binary contrast (e.g., green versus gray) that obscures the nuances of what consumers want, need, and are willing to pay for. Finally, communication that disables also includes lengthy and often inscrutable scientific discussions that are next to impossible for the average consumer to understand, never mind the manager or business leader who wants to take steps to make their business profitably sustainable.

The risks of greenwashing have triggered a pendulum swing toward greenhushing, which discourages companies from saying anything at all related to sustainability. Research from Europe found that 42 percent of "green" claims by companies were "exaggerated, false or deceptive."[29] In the summer of 2023, the European Commission planned to require companies to start substantiating claims such as "climate neutral" or "containing recycled materials."[30] The result of this scrutiny is that some companies would now rather hush their plans about their sustainability initiatives than risk being accused of greenwashing. Even the heightened scrutiny of claims—regardless of their soundness and merit—may become too much of a distraction.

Some companies have recognized that they need to turn communication from a disabler into an enabler. "Our annual sustainability report used to be 120 pages, really detailed stuff," said Tim Brooks, a vice president and the global head of sustainability at the LEGO Group. He noted that the report "is now boiled to down to 40 pages with much more accessible content and easier to read."[31]

*   *   *

More broadly speaking, sustainability is becoming synonymous with *consumer* change and not merely with *climate* change. That semantic shift has far-reaching consequences for companies that embrace it and look for ways to serve consumers quickly and at scale. For those companies, sustainability should be synonymous with exciting growth opportunities built around securing competitive advantages rather than with high costs associated with meeting or exceeding regulatory compliance requirements.

In the next chapter, we look at how the green mirage has led companies astray and prevented them from serving the high levels of pent-up consumer demand for sustainable solutions.

2   Why Companies Haven't Succeeded So Far

It is possible to quantify the difference between the green mirage and the demand revolution. Take a look at figure 2.1, which plots consumer adoption as a function of time.

The lower adoption curve in figure 2.1 reflects a belief in traditional patterns of consumer adoption. Business leaders see themselves on that curve when they believe that consumers in sufficient numbers are not willing to choose sustainable goods and services or to pay for them, despite the endless parade of sustainability advocates armed with consumer surveys that claim the opposite. These leaders buy into the green mirage by insisting that sustainability is still not a high priority for consumers where it matters commercially: at the store shelf, in the online shopping cart, or at checkout time. They believe steadfastly that a lack of a price premium means a product is not viable.

In contrast, the upper adoption curve reflects the base scenario of the demand revolution, where business leaders have the leeway to pursue consumer-driven commercial strategies that can unlock exponential growth. Solutions that meet consumers' underlying needs can follow that curve because of the pent-up demand in the market.

We refer to the shaded area between the two curves as the *perception gap*. Consumers see themselves on the upper curve, whereas companies see consumers—at best—on the lower curve. Companies that continue to believe in the green mirage are literally and figuratively behind the curve. By acting on the lower side of the perception gap, many companies are not seeing the commercial opportunities that sustainability

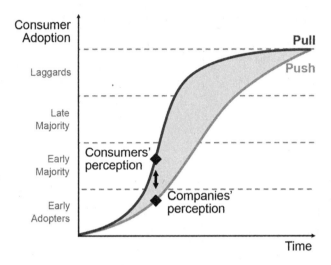

Figure 2.1
The gap between where companies believe consumers are and where they actually are.

offers, and far too few are seizing them. Nor are companies appreciating
the risks of slow action or inaction because they are too focused either
on compliance or on business decisions that seem to decouple purpose
from profit, as if the two are opposing forces. Research by First Insight
and the Baker Retailing Center at the Wharton School of the University
of Pennsylvania indicates not only that consumers and retailers are not
on the same page with respect to sustainability but also that there is
a significant disconnect between senior retail leaders and consumers.
"Not surprisingly, the sustainability imperative has been driven primarily by the consumer," the report concluded."[1]

Another factor reinforcing the perception gap is that companies
continue to measure progress with standard metrics, well known from
technology-driven megatrends and the classic innovation paradigm.
They think in terms of serving a small number of early adopters who
are most likely to understand the benefits of an innovation and pay a
premium commensurate with its perceived value. Over time, according to that principle, the company can then expand into larger market
segments.

Why Closing the Perception Gap Is Urgent

Three reasons explain why we feel that a demand-driven megatrend scales faster than a technological supply-driven megatrend, making the advantages of the upper curve in figure 2.1 substantial.

First, pent-up demand means that companies will see accelerated adoption levels and achieve clear first-mover advantages. This pent-up demand shortens the consumer learning curve and makes the megatrend transformative. It marks a fundamental difference between sustainability and other transformative megatrends. Globalization and digitalization, for example, were foreign and often intimidating when they were new. Sustainability will seem less like a stranger and more like a familiar friend when companies close their perception gap by serving the broader market of consumers. This pent-up demand for sustainable solutions has accumulated over decades.

Second, there is often a leadership vacuum regarding a sustainability positioning. In many markets, no company has become synonymous with sustainability in the eyes of consumers. When a company fills that vacuum in a trustworthy way and serves the pent-up demand, the positioning will help it achieve more rapid scaling.

The third reason is volume. Imagine if *every company* succeeded in launching a sustainable innovation in the spirit of the classic innovation paradigm. In this process, goods and services will migrate over time from niche to mainstream and from the fringes to the core business in line with the lower "push" curve in figure 2.1.[2] Yet even if that occurred, we doubt that the aggregate innovative impact would be enough to meet the world's headline sustainability targets. In other words, closing the perception gap does not express a choice but rather a reality. Without exponential growth—or at least a sharp upward trajectory in growth rates—the world will never achieve the climate-related targets expressed in international agreements.

The good news is that supply-side innovations are already having a meaningful effect in terms of reducing the world's carbon footprint. An analysis by BloombergNEF states that supply-side efforts to address environmental damage and climate change are also reaching inflection points. For the first time in 2022, the world invested as much money in replacing fossil fuels as it spent on producing oil, gas, and coal. In detail, the analysis said that "global investments in the clean energy transition hit $1.1 trillion in 2022, roughly equal to the amount invested in fossil fuel production. Never before has the amount spent on switching to renewable power, electric cars and new energy sources like hydrogen topped $1 trillion."[3]

But while making a successful energy transition on the supply side, companies cannot lose sight of the demand side. The investment community is already showing awareness of the need for that balance. "A lot of our research and investment analysis considers companies which still produce high emissions today, and assesses [whether] they really have credible and positive transition plans," said Jan-Marc Fergg, the global head of ESG and managed solutions at HSBC, "because that will give us an insight and a view around whether these companies will succeed in achieving their published or outlined net zero targets as well as their abilities in meeting customer expectations."[4]

Why Companies Struggle with Sustainable Initiatives

We assert that sustainability will be the next transformative megatrend, one that will ignite exponential growth and lead to permanent net-positive changes for a large portion of the world's population.[5] That assertion triggers two justified and fundamental questions: Why hasn't this powerful megatrend emerged yet, despite more than six decades of the modern sustainability movement? And what can companies do differently—and profitably—to accelerate progress toward the world's sustainability targets?

Some of the reasons are internal. It is hard to create a sense of urgency among internal teams when the target dates for declaring victory on some sustainability efforts are a decade or two away. The targets dates for companies to achieve net-zero carbon emissions, for example, range from 2035 to 2050. Even the most visionary leaders—especially of public companies—can struggle to keep an organization on course to a target that will likely remain unmet after the current executives have moved on. Supply-side changes, as we have said, take a long time to achieve.

The green mirage also makes it challenging for companies to set priorities because it alters the risk–reward calculus. Many of the initiatives we advocate in this book can be considered high risk because of the extent of both commercial creativity and creative destruction they require. But the green mirage turns these initiatives from "high-risk, high-reward" investments into "high-risk, iffy-reward" investments because of the limits it imposes on commercial creativity. The limitation makes the status quo or incremental changes look like better bets and leads companies to identify and pursue more "low-risk, low-reward" initiatives.

The persistence of a perception gap obscures the business cases for sustainable solutions in many sectors and has led to chronic underinvestment in sustainable solutions, in changes to go-to-market strategies, and in organizational transformations. This underinvestment has resulted in seven failure modes, shown in figure 2.2. They embed the flawed assumptions—often derived from a belief in the green mirage— that have prevented companies from unlocking commercial opportunities linked to sustainability.

These failure modes have direct consequences for consumers, who are eager and willing to respond when the right sustainable solutions become available. They don't need lectures, and they don't need scare tactics. They don't need pretty green packages or a grand ESG purpose statement. They need affordable, useful, less wasteful products at scale. They are looking to companies to provide them with solutions that will leave them with the confident belief they are making a difference and contributing to a better tomorrow, for themselves if not for society. Companies will reinforce and perpetuate these seven failure modes as long as their perceptions of consumers lag behind where consumers themselves say they are. In part III we describe how some of these failure modes affect consumer behavior. The strategic plays introduced in part IV will show how companies can avoid or overcome them.

Figure 2.2
The failure modes behind why companies haven't done enough or any sustainability work.

Green Is Gold

In this failure mode, companies overestimate the potential to charge a significant premium price for a sustainable offering and then abandon their effort when the expected revenue and profits do not materialize. The underlying assumption is that the mere presence of a sustainable feature makes a solution significantly more valuable, which justifiably warrants a significant price premium. In other cases, companies conflate willingness to pay and ability to pay and assume that even consumers on limited budgets will nonetheless pay higher prices for a desirable solution with a sustainable feature.

Some industries and categories will indeed have a small window for charging premium prices, especially to certain types of consumers. But these premiums are usually available only to first movers and only when the amounts are within consumers' affordability thresholds. At the same time, sustainability is turning into a hygiene factor for consumers, which means its presence in some form will become an expectation, not an exception. As this change unfolds, any added willingness to pay simply because something is sustainable will shrink.

If It's Green, It's Good Enough

This failure mode stems from the belief that the mere presence of a sustainable feature will attract consumers and, in some cases, warrant a premium price. This thinking often leads to products that extract a quality penalty. Instead of providing sustainable products and services that are better or on par with traditional products and services, companies provide "green" solutions that are worse in some way just so that they can keep production costs reasonable. In producing these products and services, companies make cutbacks on other consumer requirements, such as performance and convenience, because they believe that consumers will make sacrifices in order to have a sustainable solution or to take another step toward a sustainable lifestyle.

To break this failure mode, companies need to understand consumers' underlying needs and make direct links between those needs and the potential for a sustainable solution. Companies will not achieve first-mover advantages and exponential growth if they equate sustainability with consumer sacrifice and so cut corners in other areas. Only very few consumers, such as some in the archetype we call planet savers, are ready to sacrifice important attributes in a sustainable solution.

It's Only about the Message

A combination of government and corporate action over the past two decades has raised consciousness about sustainability and led to some progress on mitigating negative externalities such as greenhouse-gas emissions and other forms of pollution. In the early 2020s, however, skepticism is growing around the sincerity and feasibility of the many corporate and national commitments, with one *New York Times* editorial referring to them as "science fiction." Consumers are also increasingly skeptical about the motives behind sustainable communications.[6]

To break this failure mode, companies should recognize the extent to which many consumers are conducting their own research to verify sustainable claims. When a fashion company introduces a "green" or "eco-conscious" product line, for example, it can no longer expect consumers to take such claims at face value. Positive messaging shouldn't be a layer of green gloss over a vague promise or a way to mask a fee or surcharge. But at the same time, if companies become too stringent about the claims they make, consumers end up with less information at a time when they need more transparent, honest, and credible information. That is the risk of greenhushing, which can impede the transition to a sustainable future.

Talking Gibberish to Consumers

This is the scientific and technical counterpart to "It's only about the message." Messages about sustainability or ESG efforts may sound great in a corporate annual report, but they do not always translate well for individual consumers. That is one of the clearest findings from our focus groups and our individual interviews, as we elaborate in part III.

When companies showcase how they are mastering sustainability—whether by living up to the best practices of science-based targets or by inventing a new carbon-neutral product—they tend to get bogged down in details. Consumers often lack the time, patience, or vocabulary to decode these communications. How many consumers can make sense of a receipt that says their purchase avoided the environment's absorption of 109.14 grams of carbon dioxide (CO_2)? Most consumers, for example, have absolutely no idea what their personal carbon footprint is. This is one of a multitude of education and communication challenges that are barriers to the exponential growth that consumers can drive. But it can take time to enact uniform requirements for such labeling or disclosure. The US Department of Agriculture did not mandate detailed nutrition labels on food products until 1990.[7] When will comparable labeling show the carbon impact of other parts of day-to-day life?

The same applies to references to the Paris Agreement on climate change, the United Nations Sustainable Development Goals, carbon neutrality, carbon offsets, and net-zero emissions. Net zero, for example, is relatively easy to define at a high level. The United Nations says it means "cutting greenhouse gas emissions to as close to zero as possible, with any remaining emissions re-absorbed from the atmosphere, by oceans and forests for instance."[8] But the moment the discussion leads to the "when" and the "how," it is easy to lose the connection to consumers' day-to-day lives.

Consumers have heard too much about sustainable claims and understood too little, but the latter is not their fault. Climate change and green aspects of producing and living can be very complex, but consumers are asking companies to make it simple for them.

We Can Niche Our Way to Success

Many companies realize that they need to make changes to "business as usual" and offer sustainable solutions, often in response to pressure from governments, public opinion, investors, or their own consumers. But they often make changes on the fringes instead of pushing large-scale initiatives. They cherry-pick small sustainability initiatives, hold them at arm's length, and attempt to reap low-hanging fruit. A Euromonitor report shows that "there is an increasing risk of losing market share if a company or brand is not considered sustainable" and that "73% of businesses currently invest in sustainability to improve their brand reputation."[9] But according to three members of Capgemini Invent's Management Lab, these efforts often fall victim to "'hidden enemies' of sustainability: the prevailing organizational winds that tend to blow in the direction of routine and an incremental approach rather than sustaining a more radical and transformative journey."[10]

Making changes on the fringes is tantamount to waiting or stalling. When incumbents base their actions on how they usually innovate —test and learn on the fringes before making any big bets—they are acting too slowly. This sluggishness leaves the company vulnerable to the inherent risk that sustainable natives—companies that originate to offer sustainable solutions—will disrupt their market. To break this failure mode, companies need to decide whether they want to lead or follow in defining the sustainability standards in their industry. For smaller industry players, it can be overwhelming to make the big bets on their own, which means some will need to wait until they can follow an incumbent's lead or until they can join coalitions.

Looking to Win the Compliance Game

Governments are implementing legislation to encourage or require companies to pursue more sustainable policies. Compliance can be complicated, especially for multinational companies, because rules and requirements vary by region, by country, and, in some cases, by city. This greater regulatory burden can shift the sustainability's center of gravity in a company toward the legal department and thus even farther away from marketing and innovation, where it belongs.

Legal compliance is table stakes, but it can constrain a company when it focuses more on solutions that meet minimum standards than on treating the sustainability megatrend as an open-ended business opportunity. Such companies aim for the floor instead of for the ceiling. This strategy brings no competitive advantages and no first-mover advantages, and it leaves the company exposed to competitors that move quickly. To break this failure mode, companies should let consumers define where the ceiling for product development should be rather than letting compliance with legal requirements be the primary driver behind product development.

Playing the Waiting Game

Some companies are sitting back and waiting to see what will happen instead of swiftly taking the lead on sustainability in their industry. This approach may reflect a desire to learn from others' mistakes or from a belief that major initiatives will require joint industry effort, not the efforts of any individual company. On the one hand, smaller companies may hold the latter belief because they may lack the resources to shake up an entire industry on their own. On the other hand, a large established market leader may not want to face the short-term risks of making a bold move—say, eliminating red meat from its products or store shelves—even though it may have the leverage and the resources to reap the long-term benefits. In other cases, companies may not yet have their own profitable business case for sustainability, especially when they are trying to make the business case within the confines of the green mirage. These companies are deferring large investments until they feel the costs of developing and implementing sustainable solutions have come down.

Waiting looks like a safe and successful strategy until someone else decides not to. We highlight an example of this in part IV when we compare the decisions Fujifilm made in the early twenty-first century with the decisions Kodak made. Another risk of playing the waiting game is that a company's most potent competitor may not exist yet. In the transformative megatrend of digitalization, most of the successful companies—at least by financial and commercial measures—were megatrend natives. They did not exist before the commercial internet, nor did they have the baggage of large asset bases and business models that were designed to win in previous eras. They had the latitude to practice commercial creativity while imposing an obligation of creative destruction on others.

The Existential Challenge of Sustainability

The visceral nature of existential threats to the planet's environment lends itself to bold headlines and doomsday scenarios. These threats are not lost on the consumers we have interviewed. One of them, whom you will meet in part III, expressed this doomsday sentiment by saying that "an economy is worthless on a dead planet. I don't understand why that's not clear." Whether sustainability is an existential challenge for the planet or for humanity is vitally important, but it is not the subject of this book. We are focused instead on sustainability as an existential challenge for businesses.

Business leaders can't respond to this existential challenge until they replace the confining biases of the green mirage with the realities of the demand revolution and the opportunities it creates. If business leaders respond with urgency and creativity, the progress of the demand revolution will be virtually unstoppable because companies will have achieved the scale and the exponential growth to close the perception gap. If they fall short in this existential challenge, they will join the list of companies that have opted out of a transformative megatrend when they had the opportunities, the assets, the technologies, and the market positions to lead instead.

Figure 2.1 presents companies with a choice between three scenarios:

- **Scenario 1: Close the perception gap.** Companies meet the consumers in the marketplace by gaining a better understanding of consumers' needs and perceptions than they have today. These companies achieve speed and scale as enduring competitive advantages by identifying the largest market with the greatest readiness to purchase. They look at volume and price over time instead of homing in on the existence of a short-term premium. They find where the demand revolution is taking place, and they understand the need to fuel it. They become allies of consumers rather than looking to earn a quick buck from a nice message at the fringes of their market.

- **Scenario 2: Continue on the push curve.** If companies continue to respond to the demand revolution with only push innovations and bring them to market with the same strategic playbooks, they may continue on the push curve as a best-case scenario. But look closely at the gap between the two curves in figure 2.1. A company operating on the lower adoption curve is still marketing its innovations to early adopters at a time when a company on the upper curve is entering the equivalent of a "late-majority" phase of adoption. The competitor on the upper curve has seized a first-mover advantage that will result not only in a larger market share but also in more loyal consumers and greater means to secure and extend their competitive advantages. Pursuing scenario 2 will likely leave companies without the scale and the resources to take advantage of the demand revolution.

- **Scenario 3: Fall off the curve.** A company that launches no sustainable solutions is not participating on either curve. By betting on the status quo and ignoring or resisting the demand revolution, companies risk a worst-case scenario in which consumers eventually render them obsolete. The gap between what consumers demand and what the company offers becomes too large. These companies become victims of creative destruction rather than the makers and beneficiaries of it.

Now is the time for companies and their leaders to act. The existential challenge for business leaders boils down to two questions:

Will you be bold enough to listen to what consumers are saying about sustainability and develop solutions to meet their needs?

Or will you concede the initiative to companies that will follow a new paradigm of innovation and lock you out of the most lucrative opportunities?

The greater the pent-up demand, the larger the leadership vacuum; and the stronger a company is on the supply side, the better its chances are to capitalize on the demand revolution.

Exponential growth will remain elusive until companies recognize the perception gap, break with any failure modes they currently follow, and capitalize on the opportunities offered by the gap's upper curve. The acceleration of growth will happen when companies recognize sustainability as a commercial driver and begin to serve consumers according to the diverse needs they have rather than continue to dismiss their needs. The ones who succeed will lead a new wave of exponential growth that will over time create their own new ecosystems and once again change the lives of billions of people. That process starts with listening closely to what consumers want, what they need, and what they think.

In part II, we look at the origins of the demand revolution, the evidence behind its current trajectory, and the scale and scope of the opportunities it creates.

II The Demand Revolution: The Scope and Scale of the Strategic Opportunity

3 The Rise of the Demand Revolution

By 2024, it has become impossible to escape the ubiquitous, loud, and controversial rhetoric surrounding sustainability and the resulting debates on who should do what and by when. A statement by the English band Coldplay in the summer of 2023 is one of countless examples of how many people such rhetoric and its promises can reach with one simple message. On June 2, 2023, the band recalled this bold promise in a post to its nearly 24 million followers on Instagram: "When we first announced the Music Of The Spheres Tour [in 2021], we hoped to make it as environmentally beneficial as possible and reduce our direct carbon emissions (from production, freight, and band and crew travel) by 50%." Then the band announced that it had achieved a CO_2 reduction of 47 percent compared to its stadium tour of 2016–2017. That post received 272,000 likes and almost 2,000 comments in the following 30 days.[1]

It has taken almost 60 years to make that level of awareness commonplace. That's how far back the roots of the demand revolution stretch. To understand why the pent-up demand is high and robust in many sectors, it is worthwhile to explore how consumer wants, needs, attitudes, and behaviors have evolved over that period.

Why Sustainability Is the Next Transformative Megatrend

Our extensive research with consumers over the past several years indicates that sustainability will soon evolve from an important purchase criterion into a hygiene factor. The first movers will have the opportunity to create enduring competitive advantages and high entry barriers built around consumer loyalty. "I think there will be a market at some point where customers would just say 'if you cannot give me green, don't even show up,'" said Vincent Clerc, the CEO of the global shipping giant A.P. Moller–Maersk.[2]

Sustainability will be the next transformative megatrend, one on par with previous ones such as digitalization, globalization, mass production, and electrification. To sharpen this statement, it would help to have a definition of "megatrends" and an understanding of when they become transformative. John Naisbitt introduced the term *megatrends* and defined them as "large social, economic, political, and technological changes [that] are slow to form, and once in place, they influence us for some time—between seven and ten years, or longer."[3] Andrew Winston, who wrote the books *Green to Gold* and *The Big Pivot*, used the term *gigatrends* to describe forces or trends that involve billions of units (such as carbon) and require large investments that will affect billions of people.[4] Stefan Hajkowicz, a scientist at Australia's Commonwealth Scientific and Industrial Research Organisation, proposed defining megatrends more provocatively as "gradual yet powerful trajectories of change that will at some point express themselves with explosive force and throw companies, individuals and societies into freefall."[5] We feel that Hajkowicz's definition is more appropriate for describing what is happening with sustainability, though we don't expect a freefall as an inevitable consequence. We expect the opposite.

Previous transformative megatrends originated from landmark innovations and a series of technological shifts that altered the way people went about their lives. That process is what we refer to as "push" innovation, when a company either senses unmet consumer needs or has a new technology that it is confident it can build a market around. Technological push helped companies such as Amazon, Apple, Ford, and many others trigger exponential growth in industries that created massive ecosystems and changed the lives of billions of people. Most major business revolutions have had their roots in push innovation, regardless of whether they resulted in transformative megatrends. In the biography *Steve Jobs*, the late Apple CEO described this philosophy: "Some people say, 'Give the customers what they want.' But that's not my approach. Our job is to figure out what they're going to want before they do. I think Henry Ford once said, 'If I'd asked customers what they wanted, they would have told me, 'A faster horse!' People don't know what they want until you show it to them. That's why I never rely on market research. Our task is to read things that are not yet on the page."[6]

With few exceptions, the innovations from this push or supply-side thinking usually need a longer time for mass adoption because consumers need to learn how and why to change their behavior significantly. The idealized "push" mentality seeks to develop solutions that are beyond the imagination of consumers rather than coincide with their imagination.

That thinking also occurred with the globalization megatrend. Consumers needed to learn and trust that quality goods could come reliably and consistently from another continent. European and American consumers, for example, needed to adapt and acknowledge that quality products could come from Asian countries. Another example is e-commerce under the digitalization megatrend. Consumers needed to adapt to buying products online, which marked a significant change in purchasing behavior. Several years later, we saw the controversial shock of COVID-19 accelerate e-commerce.

So, in contrast, what would a business revolution based on consumer-led "pull" look like? Imagine that consumers articulate a demand for a different future and not only a better present. They claim some responsibility for taking their destinies into their own hands, but those claims are not empty rhetoric on the bandwagon of a new megatrend. Instead, consumers are backing up the claims with a willingness to vote with their money to make the business revolution succeed.

How would Apple's iPhone or Ford's Model T have succeeded if the pent-up demand for their breakthrough products were clearer, but the market was historically underserved because no one wanted to take the risk and place big bets? Apple and Ford could have acted with even more certainty and less risk in such a situation. That is the situation that we believe exists right now with respect to sustainability: pent-up demand in historically underserved or poorly served markets.

The Roots of the Demand Revolution

How can sustainability be touted as the defining issue of the early and mid-twenty-first century when there is not even a consensus on how to define the term?

The United Nations website posted a statement in 2023 after the release of the latest climate report from the Intergovernmental Panel on Climate Change (IPCC). "UN Secretary-General António Guterres said that the IPCC report launched today is 'a clarion call to massively fast-track climate efforts by every country and every sector and on every timeframe.'" In a reference to the film that won the Academy Award for Best Picture in 2023, Guterres added that "our world needs climate action on all fronts—'everything, everywhere, all at once.'"[7]

Guterres's call to action may sound urgent and dramatic, but it is in fact nothing new. To put his plea into context, let's look at how these calls to action have evolved since awareness about climate change and sustainability first reached the mainstream in the 1960s. From the beginning, the high-level logic behind sustainable innovation has been simple: mitigating or eliminating negative externalities is essential to improving people's lives. These negative externalities include greenhouse-gas emissions, ocean and groundwater pollution, food waste, deforestation, and solid-waste disposal. Thanks to the accumulated impact of those externalities, human beings now live in what Justin McGuirk, the chief curator at the Design Museum in London, refers to as the Waste Age.[8]

To explore the contradictions and controversies around sustainability and to establish a working definition of *sustainability*, we highlight four influential publications, one from each of the last four decades of the twentieth century. Three of those publications were best-selling books that energized and polarized public opinion in their own ways. Over time, the collective weight of the sentiments expressed in these land-mark books—as well as in countless other publications over the past 60 years—has fundamentally changed the way consumers consume. Our measurement and interpretation of those numerous and nuanced changes—which form the core of part III of our book—lay the ground-work for the strategic framework we introduce in part IV that will enable companies across all industries and all regions to respond to those new behavioral and consumption patterns at scale and with speed.

The seeds of the demand revolution have been sprouting for decades. Rachel Carson's book *Silent Spring*, published in 1962, "led to an increased public awareness of humanity's impact on nature and is credited as the beginning of the modern environmental movement, leading to the establishment of the Environmental Protection Agency in 1970 and the banning of DDT in 1972," according to the Smithson-ian Institution.[9]

The sustainability movement received a powerful jolt when the Club of Rome published *Limits of Growth* in 1972. That best-selling book rested on the premise that "if the present growth trends in population, industrialisation, pollution, food production, and resource depletion continue unchanged, the limits to growth on this planet will be reached sometime within the next one hundred years. The most probable result will be a rather sudden and uncontrollable decline in both population and industrial capacity." Despite this bleak outlook, the book's research team, which included several scientists from the Massachusetts Insti-tute of Technology (MIT), also argued that people have the capacity to "alter these growth trends and to establish a condition of ecological and economic stability that is sustainable far into the future."[10]

In 1987, the Brundtland Commission, an organization within the United Nations, published the report *Our Common Future*. It clearly and succinctly stated that sustainable development "meets the needs of the present without compromising the ability of future generations to meet their own needs."[11] We base our definition of environmental sustainability on the Brundtland publication: products and services are sustainable if they meet current needs *and* if their direct and indirect impacts will not diminish the opportunities of future generations.

In 1992, future US vice president Al Gore published the best-selling book *Earth in the Balance: Forging a New Common Purpose*. In a later edition, Gore said that he could not have "predicted how long it would take for the scientific consensus to solidify." He continued, "The nature and severity of the climate crisis had seemed painfully obvious to me for quite a long time; but in retrospect, I wish we could have had in the 1990's the deafening scientific consensus that has emerged in more recent years." He also reiterated his conclusion from the first edition: "We can believe in [the] future and work to achieve it and preserve it, or we can whirl blindly on, behaving as if one day there will be no children to inherit our legacy."[12]

These publications promised a wave of sweeping change—a transformative megatrend—that has yet to materialize.

In contrast to the world's previous transformative megatrends—such as mass production, electrification, globalization, and digitalization—the forces behind the innovations that will power the sustainability megatrend will not originate primarily or solely from a strong technological push in the spirit of Edison, Ford, or Jobs. They will instead originate from a strong consumer pull, which is already underway.

*   *   *

A sense of sustainability—specifically environmental sustainability—now permeates the thinking of a critical mass of consumers to such an extent that it is now a fundamental purchase criterion alongside price, quality, and brand. It has begun to change the way consumers behave and the way they consume and has generated the pent-up demand we describe in chapter 4.

4 The Evidence of a Consumer-Driven Megatrend

Research by New York University's Stern Center for Sustainable Business showed that sales of products marketed as sustainable have grown 5.6 times faster than those that were not. In more than 90 percent of the consumer-packaged goods categories, sustainability-marketed products grew faster than their conventional counterparts.[1]

Data from other industries also provides evidence that pent-up demand exists and that alternative consumption patterns have been emerging for several years. The growth in renewable energy has far exceeded expectations since the first projections of capacity in 2006. The 2030 projections for solar power capacity are 30 times higher compared to 2006 projections and four times higher for wind onshore- and offshore-capacity projections.[2] This evidence of rapid scaling is important. In its *Energy Source* newsletter in June 2023, the *Financial Times* addressed one aspect of sustainability—the necessary shift away from fossil fuels—and stated that "capitalism won't deliver the energy transition fast enough. . . . There's too much to do, and given the urgency and the need to get the solution right, this isn't a task for your favourite ESG-focused portfolio manager or the tech bros. The sheer scale of the physical infrastructure that must be revamped, demolished or replaced is almost beyond comprehension."[3] The newsletter called for the sustainability equivalent of a Marshall Plan, the US-led plan to rebuild Europe after World War II.

The growth in the EV market also indicates pent-up demand. Boston Consulting Group (BCG) regularly makes detailed projections for

the adoption of EVs by the year 2030. These kinds of optimistic forecasts are fodder for skeptics, though, who are eager to dismiss widely
hyped innovations as passing trends or to see exponential growth as
a fantasy because so much can happen over the course of a decade or
more. BCG has indeed felt compelled to revise its rosy forecasts every
year, but not in the way the skeptics anticipated. The firm has in fact
revised the projections *upward* each year as the demand for EVs accelerated more quickly than expected. Its projection for the EV market
share in the United States in 2030 progressively increased from 22 percent in 2018 to 53 percent in 2022, as shown in figure 2.1. For the
global market, BCG projected the 2030 global EV market share to be
20 percent in 2018 and 44 percent in 2022. BCG has acknowledged the
need for a significant revision: "In fact, our updated forecast predicts
that by 2026 electrified vehicles will account for more than half of
light vehicles sold globally—four years sooner than we anticipated in
our previous report."[4] We see the consistent upward revisions as additional evidence of pent-up consumer demand. In this case, it should
convince automotive OEMs that they should make larger investments in the EV market or risk leaving a commercial opportunity on
the table.[5]

A critical mass of consumers now feels they have personal agency
over the kind of world they want to live in and leave behind. They
want to spend their money on goods and services that will help them
create that world. As they articulate their needs regarding sustainability,
they are developing breakthrough habits, changing their attitudes, and
redefining expectations.

Our research shows that this megatrend derives to a far greater
extent from consumer demand—or consumer "pull"—than from the
"push" of technological invention. We refer to this pull effect as a
"demand revolution" because of its speed and scale. The push effect
remains essential, but the pull provides the necessary focus, direction,
and inspiration to maximize the effects of the push. Consumers see
themselves on a different adoption curve—with a much faster and

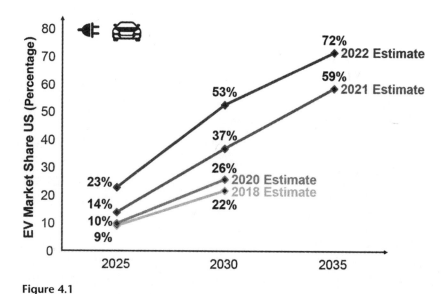

Figure 4.1

BCG has consistently revised its estimates of EV penetration by 2030 to reflect high demand. *Sources*: Figure drawn from data given in Boston Consulting Group (BCG), "The Electric Car Tipping Point," 2018, https://web-assets.bcg.com/ef/8b /007df7ab420dab1164e89d0a6584/bcg-the-electric-car-tipping-point-jan-2018 .pdf; BCG, "Who Will Drive Electric Cars to the Tipping Point?," 2020, https:// www.bcg.com/publications/2020/drive-electric-cars-to-the-tipping-point; BCG, "Why Electric Cars Can't Come Fast Enough," 2021, https://www.bcg.com /publications/2021/why-evs-need-to-accelerate-their-market-penetration; BCG, "Electric Cars Are Finding Their Next Gear," 2022, https://www.bcg.com/pub lications/2022/electric-cars-finding-next-gear.

higher growth trajectory—than the adoption curve that companies currently see because they underestimate the size of the markets for sustainable solutions.

We want to show not only that this pent-up consumer demand exists but also how diverse consumers are in their wants, needs, and willingness to pay. This doesn't mean they will automatically pay a premium or make a sacrifice. The demand instead raises the possibility that they will buy frequently, consistently, and loyally—three themes that came out strongly in the consumer research we feature in part III.

The Basis for Our New Strategic Framework

After years of dismissing sustainability's potential as a commercial opportunity, business leaders may be surprised to see how far advanced consumers are in their thinking. Consumers know what they want. They are ready to spend money on the right solutions, and they will be loyal to the companies that meet their wants and needs. In detail, we base our arguments for the demand revolution on insights drawn from four sources: large-scale consumer research, consumer focus groups and interviews, executive interviews, and third-party research.[6]

Large-Scale Consumer Research

Simon-Kucher conducted extensive quantitative surveys on sustainability in 2021 and 2022 with around 8,000 consumers in Europe and North America.[7] Hereafter, we refer to these two surveys as the "core studies." This database provided input for the advanced statistical analyses that revealed patterns, relationships, and trends in consumer behavior with respect to sustainability. These analyses also yielded a segmentation with eight distinct archetypes of consumers, each with its own behaviors, attitudes, biases, needs, expectations, and willingness to pay. Conducting the surveys in consecutive years allowed the observation of year-over-year changes and led to conclusions about the future evolution of each consumer archetype as well as the stability of the core findings amid different macroeconomic and geopolitical conditions.

Consumer Focus Groups and Interviews

We conducted seven focus groups—one for each consumer archetype (except for the nonbelievers)—with more than 70 consumers in the United States. We then supplemented the focus groups with interviews with one participant representing each archetype. The focus groups and follow-up interviews provided valuable qualitative insights from the consumer perspective because they gave us a detailed view of the individual's current opinions, attitudes, and day-to-day experiences with sustainability. They allowed us to develop a sharper and richer picture of each archetype based on a deeper understanding of their nuances.

Executive Interviews

We conducted in-depth interviews with executives across industries in both the business-to-consumer and business-to-business sectors. These executives provided alternative viewpoints and insights into their companies' strategies and their own decision-making processes.

Third-Party Research

We have used a wide range of third-party findings and insights to supplement and challenge our own research. They include studies, analyses, and projections from public and private organizations, academics, journalists, consulting firms, and other subject-matter experts.

How Consumers Are Exerting a Strong Pull on Markets

One sign of the strong pull is that consumers are already looking for alternative ways to meet their needs in the absence of solutions from companies. The forms and extent of these actions vary from consumer to consumer in line with the eight archetypes of consumers that we introduce in part III.

Numerous sources—from qualitative and quantitative studies and interviews to project experience and third-party research—have revealed that consumer spending is changing in several ways, each with specific implications for companies' commercial strategies. Figure 4.2 shows seven of these major trends. We are not portraying these trends as new. Rather, we are showing current consumer perceptions of them and highlighting corporate efforts to follow these paths. Companies need to decide which path is the one of least resistance as they develop their own commercial strategies for sustainability. Without accelerated or greater scale, these paths are not sufficient—individually or collectively—to achieve exponential growth. The perpetuation of the failure modes, especially the emphasis on messaging or green

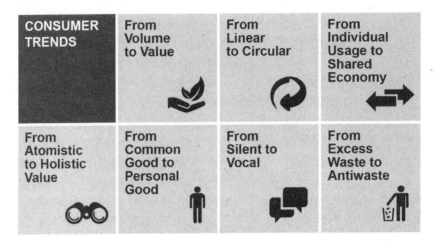

Figure 4.2
Seven examples of consumer pull for sustainable solutions.

premium, will all but ensure that companies never achieve the necessary scale.

From Volume to Value

Consumers are moving away from low-quality, short-lifetime unsustainable products toward longer-lasting products, even if the latter are more expensive. This means companies will need to replace "planned obsolescence" or "design for failure" with a "design to last" philosophy. Allied Research and Research and Markets have projected that the luxury-apparel market will have an annualized growth rate of 13.1 percent through the year 2026, far ahead of the annual growth rate of 7.9 percent projected for fast fashion in the same period.[8] "If you as a company make a quality product that can last a long time, I think you are still the most sustainable," said Henk de Jong, the CEO of Versuni (formerly Philips Domestic Appliances).[9] Recycling and upgrading become extremely important, however, in a market characterized by rapid innovation. Some products with longer shelf lives could become obsolete before breaking down.

For consumers, longevity often means a higher upfront cost but lower operating costs because there is less maintenance, no replacement, and better residual value at the end of the lifecycle. The US-based manufacturer Ariat, which we explore further in chapter 13, aims for this appeal in its boots and other leather products.

From Linear to Circular

End-to-end sustainability follows a product through its conception and creation, consumption, reuse, disposal, and ultimately recycling of as much of its constituent material as possible. The result over time is less use of virgin raw materials, less production, and less energy consumption.

The shift from linear to circular is underway in several industries, ranging from consumer electronics to fashion. The worldwide revenue of secondhand apparel has tripled in the past decade, reaching $43 billion in 2022, according to thredUP.[10] Awareness campaigns such as Overshoot Day attempt to encourage consumers to move away from industries such as fast fashion and to shop instead at their local or digital thrift store. "Our perception is that if you have to make the most sustainable choice, it is probably going to be a secondhand choice," said Andrea Baldo, the CEO of the high-end Danish fashion company GANNI. "We see a reduction in rental frequency, that's for sure," he added. "We see secondhand booming more." Baldo compares the rise of the sustainability megatrend with the rise of e-commerce, but the required changes are more extensive than making greater investments in sustainable solutions. Sustainability "needs to be embedded into the business model," he said. "It's not about spending more money or finding more solutions," which, he believes, is too simple and short-sighted.[11]

GANNI's circular business model, called GANNI Repeat, encompasses resale, rental, recycling, and repair. To incentivize customers to return clothing, it offers store credits, which customers can use immediately to buy other secondhand products. This strategy allows a high-end company such as GANNI to attract more price-sensitive consumers. The company has also calculated that the value of these secondhand consumers extends beyond the individual transaction as they become advocates and allow GANNI to capitalize on network effects. "A lot more customers are making smart choices, but they are making smart choices based on the budget they have," Baldo said. "They are not increasing their budget to make smart choices." Nonetheless, GANNI sees that its products still attract a sort of green premium on the secondhand market relative to products that were not made as responsibly.

GANNI also sees differences across secondhand channels. The online market tends to focus more on unique products or occasions, while the secondhand market encourages more of a true community effect. Consumers personally bring their clothes to the GANNI stores for exchange and tend to buy more commercial products.

The World Economic Forum has estimated that around 50 percent of the world's greenhouse gas emissions result from the extraction and processing of natural resources. Under a "business-as-usual" scenario, it forecasts that demand for raw materials will double by 2050. A separate estimate claims that the world consumed 1.75 times the earth's regenerative resources in 2022. Such data points prompted the forum to assert that "business-as-usual is not an option" as the 2030 deadline looms for achieving the United Nations Sustainable Development Goals.[12]

The efforts by GANNI show what companies can achieve when they change their business models to focus more on the commercial side of sustainability. But Tjeerd Jegen, the former CEO of the Dutch retail chain HEMA, sees the need for industry-wide initiatives. "Circularity must be driven and supported by the industry," he said. "The 'every man for himself' game isn't going to work." He feels that the consumer trend toward circularity will determine the future for retailers and that they will be forced to prioritize sustainability in order to be successful.[13]

From Individual Usage to Shared Economy

From cars to clothes to power equipment, many goods that consumers own will sit idle for the vast majority of the goods' useful lives.

But thanks to innovators from Uber to Airbnb to Rent the Runway, consumers can now make an increasing number of "buy or borrow" decisions in their daily lives.[14] The growth of borrowing—known commonly as the "sharing economy"—makes a significant contribution to sustainability because it uses fewer resources more efficiently. It plays an important role in the demand revolution because it offers consumers a range of benefits that go beyond sustainability. Whether it means easier access, more choices, or better quality, consumers can often derive greater value in the sharing economy than they can from traditional ownership.

The transportation industry is seen as one of the world's worst carbon emitters, responsible for more than 16 percent of global greenhouse-gas emissions.[15] Consumers' awareness about the negative impact of their mobility activity—along with price, access, and convenience—has resulted in increased engagement in shared-mobility services. Statista forecasts the shared-mobility market to grow annually by 4 percent through 2027, while it expects the market for conventional passenger cars to shrink by 0.1 percent annually over the same period.[16] Many consumers are now choosing to rent out their own residence and to stay in a private residence while on vacation, taking advantage of platforms such as Airbnb, which tripled its annual revenue between 2017 and 2022.[17]

From Atomistic to Holistic Value

Try to list all the discrete steps in the value chain to get food from the farm to your table as a finished meal or all the steps the material in your garments undergo between the cotton field and your closet. The list will probably be long, and the odds are high that you have left out a few steps.

Many products pass through several intermediate steps before they reach the consumer. Consumers must then engage in a series of steps to derive value from the goods they purchase. A holistic value chain or ecosystem optimizes the use of intermediaries and allows consumers the most direct and efficient access to what they want. Done right, it offers them more choices and more value with less waste. When measured across multiple activities and large geographical areas, the savings from such collectively outsourced experiences—and thus the contribution to sustainability—can be enormous at scale.

By buying directly from manufacturers, consumers cut out intermediaries and receive better prices, faster delivery, and personal service. Technology has allowed many smaller companies to sell online, further increasing consumer choice and flexibility. A forecast from eMarketer expects direct-to-consumer e-commerce sales to grow by 22.7 percent annually through 2024.[18]

The trend from atomistic to holistic value also encompasses the shift from global to local production. The concept of comparative advantage helped drive the globalization megatrend by shifting the production of goods to countries or regions with low labor costs and better access to resources. As the Organization for Economic Cooperation and Development described in a report in 2011, the concept "posits that all economies have trade opportunities to exploit and these opportunities stem from differences in factor endowments between countries. [It] continues to be one of the most potent explanations of higher income growth in open economies."[19]

But one widely accepted downside of globalization is the carbon emissions from long-distance transportation. To the extent that such emissions affect consumers' choices of which product to buy, companies will need to determine which model is more sustainable: global shipping from centralized production or local shipping to target consumers from decentralized production. This topic was top of mind for our focus-group participants in the United States, one of whom said that "companies have to do more. It's on their shoulders if they are recycling their waste and the way they decide to ship."

This applies to where consumers shop as well as what they buy. UK residents have begun shopping closer to home.[20] The consumer preference for shopping locally is also evident in the Netherlands, according to Marit van Egmond, the CEO of Albert Heijn. "It's important where the products come from, as the demand for closer to home is growing."[21]

From Common Good to Personal Good

Sustainability is often associated with the need for collective action, with responses that require individuals to subjugate their needs to a common goal. This perspective is independent of whether they see societal benefit as something in their own self-interest. But perspectives from consumers show that they want to experience and perceive a clear difference in the goods and services they buy rather than feeling they must sacrifice today for a benefit that is far in the future. This means that companies need to communicate not only how their products and services contribute to a common goal but also how the individual consumer's contribution matters.

"I'm very conscious of the kinds of things that I'm putting into my body and my daughter's body," said one of the focus-group participants, who also provided an interview featured in part III. Many of the participants across all the consumer archetypes drew a similar link between sustainability and health or, more broadly, between sustainability and how it makes them and their families better off. The effects on society, although positive, are a secondary motivation.

Cosmetics and personal-care products are an important sector in this regard because consumers are becoming more aware of the effects that potentially harmful substances and chemicals can have. This awareness has contributed to the growth of natural and organic products, which represented roughly 7 percent of the total personal-care market in 2021. Statista predicts that the organic and natural beauty market is expected to outgrow the market for conventional products by 40 percent from 2020 to 2027.[22]

Food production accounts for 26 percent of all greenhouse-gas emissions worldwide. Many consumers have changed their consumption patterns not only by moving away from emission-heavy products such as meat but also by moving toward more holistically sustainable ones, such as organically produced products. From 2014 to 2021, the market share of organic food sales in the United States increased from 4.9 percent to 6.4 percent. The annual growth rate was 6.9 percent, more than double the overall market growth rate of 2.9 percent.[23]

From Silent to Vocal

The transformative megatrend of digitalization has left consumers more interconnected than ever before. By 2019, more than half of the global population was connected to the internet, thanks in large part to the ubiquitous mobile phone.

E-commerce data, some of which we have cited already, shows the extent to which people are using this newfound connectivity to shop. But more importantly—and perhaps more insidiously—for companies that sell to consumers, some people are using the connectivity to share their experiences with goods and services to such an extent that they have spawned a new vernacular featuring terms such as *influencers*, *brand ambassadors*, *advocates*, *digital creators*, and *greenfluencers*.

The combined extent and power of these networks was one of the most profound findings from the focus groups and in the personal interviews with consumers. It seems that consumers give little weight to the communications strategies from a brand or an organization— many of which cost millions of dollars to create and disseminate— unless friends, family, neighbors, social media contacts, and influencers have filtered the content and either endorsed it or dismissed it. Many of the consumers, in turn, aspire to be that influential friend or neighbor by informing others about their experiences. In March 2023, the consumer-products giant Unilever cited study data that underscored the influence of social media on consumers. "Three in four people (75%) are more likely to take up behaviours to help save the planet after watching social media content about sustainability," the company reported, adding that "eight in ten (83%) think TikTok and Instagram are good places to get advice about how to live sustainably."[24] Companies such as Patagonia, Lush, and adidas have undertaken campaigns to use influencers to guide consumer behavior, directly or indirectly.

Beyond this form of grassroots sharing of experiences, the number of published online reviews has also increased exponentially. According to research published in *Forbes*, the number of reviews increased by 75 percent for shaving and grooming products, 84 percent for facial-care products, and by 257 percent for verified purchases of facial-care products.[25]

From Excess Waste to Antiwaste

Waste is an issue that is so powerful that reducing or eliminating it appeals even to consumers who challenge the science behind the effects of climate change. "It's just this general aversion to being wasteful," said one of our focus-group participants as he drew a distinction in his personal life between supporting conservation (which he does) and believing claims about climate change (which he doubts). "I don't know what the motivation is, but it's not necessarily money or my own well-being or even not necessarily thinking about the planet or others well-being," he elaborated.

One common target for reducing waste is packaging. The US Environmental Protection Agency estimated in 2018 that more than 28 percent of all municipal solid waste in the United States came from packaging.[26] That estimate predates the surge in deliveries of packages during the pandemic, when online ordering boomed.[27] "We have to take into account everything that is part of buying clothes, such as packaging, hooks and bags," explained Giny Boer, the CEO of the apparel company C&A. "We need to eliminate the use of 'virgin plastic' throughout the supply chains of apparel producers."[28] Some 43 percent of consumers say that sustainable packaging is important to them when shopping.[29]

Food is another area of excessive waste. In the United States, more than one-third of all available food goes uneaten through loss or waste, according to the US Department of Agriculture, which creates a challenge for consumers to go from overconsumption to optimal consumption.[30] Consumers are interested in both the time benefits and economical savings of "ready-to-cook" meal kits, but the market growth also embodies sustainability aspects such as food-waste reduction. They are moving away from the traditional atomistic "do-everything-yourself" toward holistic package solutions that embody new values such as sustainability. Grand View Research forecasts that the meal-kit service market will grow by 17 percent annually through 2030.[31]

Another problem with food production is that it is optimized for the supermarket shelf rather than for the consumer. It must be easy to ship and easy to stock and must be encased in plastic or other materials so that it doesn't break or leak or spoil quickly. These processes generate a great deal of material waste and result in food waste when retailers need to dispose of products that are past their expiration or "sell by" dates.

Finally, antiwaste has a universal appeal. Around 15 percent of the consumer population in Europe and North America falls into an archetype we call "nonbelievers." They do not see sustainability as a meaningful influence in their lives, nor are they prepared to pay any premium at all for sustainable solutions. But many of them expressly hate waste, and that is their contribution—willing or not—to the world's progress toward sustainability goals.

*   *   *

The core studies and focus groups revealed that if consumers lack accessible or satisfactory sustainable products, many of them will either consume less or alter their spending patterns as they seek alternative solutions to meet their needs. They connect sustainability not only with decreasing waste and improving the use and conservation of society's resources but also with improving their own health and well-being. They are reluctantly accepting a quality penalty.

Taken to its extreme, this behavioral change poses a high risk across all product categories, even necessities such as groceries. Consumers are taking sustainability into their own hands—albeit reluctantly for some—by aiming to become more self-reliant. This aim manifests itself in growing some of their own food, repurposing products, deferring large purchases, and making other trade-offs that may seem noble but really represent sacrifices in the absence of better sustainable solutions from companies. It also creates a risk for established companies because they may not be able to respond to pent-up consumer demand as quickly as disruptive newcomers or "sustainability natives" will.

Underestimating demand is one reason why businesses and governments have enacted too many low-risk, low-reward solutions. They struggle to make the kinds of bold changes that will result in exponential growth in part because they don't see the pent-up demand and the behavioral changes that are driving it.

The evidence we presented in this chapter should also serve as a powerful motivation for companies to change the way they innovate and then take their innovations to market to generate the exponential growth that will power both the sustainability megatrend and their own profitable sustainable futures. In the next chapter, we look at the scale and scope of this opportunity.

5 The Scope and Scale of the Strategic Opportunity

Sustainability becomes a source of enduring competitive advantage when a company achieves a first-mover advantage at scale and builds on the increased consumer stickiness and loyalty that the first-mover advantage confers.

Put another way, we contend that companies at the forefront of this transformative megatrend will achieve long-lasting competitive advantages by investing in sustainability with speed and scale, facilitated by innovative business models that will create high entry barriers for potential competitors. They need to pursue competitive advantage instead of compliance advantage.

The Benefits of Moving First and Moving Fast

An article in *Harvard Business Review* defined a first-mover advantage as "a firm's ability to be better off than its competitors as a result of being first to market in a new product category."[1] The benefits of a first-mover advantage include:

- **Long-lived market share:** Companies that are first to market typically capture a larger market share compared to later entrants. One study found that an early market leader, defined as the "firm that is the market share leader during the early growth phase of the product life cycle," achieves a mean market share of 28 percent.[2]
- **Brand recognition:** First-mover entrants can build their brand names and obtain a strong market position. In a global study by Ipsos, some

73 percent of respondents said they are more likely to trust a brand they know.[3] Yet when we asked our focus-group participants if they could name a brand that they trusted to deliver sustainable solutions across different product categories, they were unable to do so in the vast majority of the cases. This supports our assertion that most sectors still have no true owner of sustainability leadership. First movers can seize that position. First movers such as Patagonia in sustainable outdoor wear and Tesla in electric vehicles "own" the sustainability position in their industries.

- **Learning curve:** The first mover can gather valuable supply-side experience that can lead to additional insights and knowledge about the market, the customers, and the industry. GANNI's CEO Andrea Baldo stressed this point about sustainability: "It's a matter to start now to experiment and understand how to integrate in the business model." Henk de Jong, the CEO of Versuni, noted that "we really think that sustainability is test and learn. Test and learn."[4]

- **Network effects:** In certain cases, a first mover can also create network effects that are difficult for competitors to replicate. These network effects can arise from how consumers talk about the solutions and not necessarily from something intrinsic in the solutions themselves.

Several companies continue to benefit from the value and longevity of their early successes decades after their market entry: Coca-Cola in soft drinks, Gillette in safety razors, and Sony in personal stereo equipment.[5] To achieve first-mover advantages, companies need to invest ahead of the inflection point in order to be ready to accelerate when the market shifts and makes rapid mass adoption possible.

In contrast to previous technology-driven megatrends, the primary driver of the sustainability megatrend is consumer demand. Figure 5.1 shows how these two kinds of megatrends differ. We qualify our definition of first-mover advantage by adding speed and scale. This is another difference between the traditional playbooks and paradigms

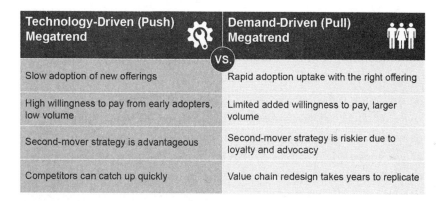

Technology-Driven (Push) Megatrend	Demand-Driven (Pull) Megatrend
Slow adoption of new offerings	Rapid adoption uptake with the right offering
High willingness to pay from early adopters, low volume	Limited added willingness to pay, larger volume
Second-mover strategy is advantageous	Second-mover strategy is riskier due to loyalty and advocacy
Competitors can catch up quickly	Value chain redesign takes years to replicate

Figure 5.1
The inherent differences between previous technology-driven megatrends and a demand-driven megatrend.

for innovation and the new innovation paradigm we advocate. Companies using conventional models can afford to target early adopters and wait on the rest of the market because they can charge considerable price premiums. They can afford a skimming strategy, even for an extended period, before penetrating the market after they have saturated the early adopters and earned back much of their initial investment. In contrast, the go-to-market strategies for sustainable solutions will need to rely heavily on a penetration strategy instead of a skimming strategy. We are not recommending that companies forgo a green premium in their market if such a premium does indeed exist. Instead, we are tempering expectations about the extent and the durability of green premiums and recommending that companies achieve larger volumes as soon as they can.

The Simon-Kucher core studies in 2021–2022 confirmed that a willingness to pay a premium for sustainability exists among *some* consumers, but it is by no means widespread.[6] Overall, we expect this willingness to pay to decline, which intensifies the urgency for companies to act now to achieve the necessary scale to serve consumers over the long term by developing sustainable solutions at lower costs and at scale.

The Benefits of Greater Loyalty, Advocacy, and Share of Wallet

Our research shows that companies providing sustainable products and services will achieve a more loyal customer base and gain opportunities for an increasing share of wallet by offering other solutions.

A TrendSights Analysis on sustainability and ethics reported that 56 percent of consumers are more loyal to brands that support "green" or environmental matters, while 58 percent will buy more products from a brand if it aligns with their personal beliefs and values.[7] A *Forbes* article claimed in early 2021 that 68 percent of consumers plan to step up their efforts to identify brands that reduce environmental impact.[8] Those findings are in line with the behaviors of our focus-group participants and their own commitments to researching sustainable brands. The majority of the focus-group participants said that they would be more loyal to a sustainable brand than to a nonsustainable brand.

One reason why consumers become more loyal to sustainable companies and their products is that, unlike for normal purchases, for sustainable purchases they spend considerably more time going through an extended purchasing journey to ensure a company is truly sustainable. They absorb more information and take more time to weigh alternatives. This process builds up their trust and confidence in the sustainable brands they do select, leading to a top-of-mind position the next time they make a purchase. They do not need to embark on a new extended purchasing journey. A common motivation between the company and the consumer—such as a shared purpose in the spirit of "doing good"—can enhance this loyalty, as we discuss in part IV when we describe the brand play in chapter 13.

This loyal customer base creates opportunities for up- and cross-selling. Brands that own the sustainability agenda in their industries can use that positioning to sustain their competitive advantages. This loyalty can also amplify the network effects of advocacy. Loyal supporters who continue to have positive experiences with a product or service tend to tell others about it, whether they talk to friends and neighbors, write an online review, or post on social media. These forms of communication are the primary information sources for many consumers, as we observe in detail in part III.

Loyalty and scale help companies create and defend barriers to entry. When companies adopt the new innovation paradigm to meet consumers' sustainability needs, it will be difficult for competitors to replicate it, at least in the short to midterm. Combined with scale, this replication barrier reinforces the enduring competitive advantage by allowing the company to serve consumers at lower costs than competitors.

Even energy companies, which often face a challenging transition because of their large investments in nonsustainable assets, have witnessed both the rapid onset of the sustainability megatrend and the benefits that arise from responding quickly. "I thought we would ride a wave of 12 meters, and now we're sitting on a wave of 20 meters," said Leonhard Birnbaum, the CEO of the German energy company E.ON. He was describing for us the unexpectedly rapid emergence of sustainability as a business opportunity. Sustainability represents a challenging transition for energy companies because executives such as Birnbaum need to strike the right balance between commercial creativity and creative destruction. One mitigating factor is regulation. Sustainability means that E.ON is "looking at a decade of growth, regulated growth, because it's a regulated business." The investment requirements are substantial, but Birnbaum is not shying away from them because he believes that sustainability is good business. "There is no energy transition without us, so it's actually a huge opportunity," he explained. "Our strategy is pretty straightforward. We have a megatrend that is driving a decade of growth. We want to capture that growth." Research has shown that E.ON's efforts are succeeding. It has experienced higher stickiness with sustainable consumers for several reasons. "You have high lock-in value, basically no churn, and you know that means that you have low cost-to-serve and you can make a decent margin also on those customers."[9]

You might recall the *Financial Times* comment we quoted in chapter 4, which said that private companies could not accomplish the energy transition because "the sheer scale of the physical infrastructure that must be revamped, demolished or replaced is almost beyond compre-hension."[10] Birnbaum is not discouraged by such sentiments. "Where do you get an infinite amount of capital? That is actually no problem," he said. "You just need to provide a good business case. Then you get the money. So for me it is important that we make it a business." Birn-baum feels he and his company have made the business case, but now they need to implement that case successfully. "All our attention is on how we can deliver, and then automatically we are doing great on ESG, digitization, growth . . . and shareholder return," he said. "It's not really rocket science anymore. Now it's all about delivery. The only thing that matters is delivery."

*   *   *

Consumers are the essence of the demand revolution. In part III, we go far beyond the simplistic view of the green mirage and introduce a detailed segmentation of consumers. But this is more than a recitation of research. We show how the consumer archetypes we have uncovered are the wellspring for sustainable solutions that are affordable, acces-sible, and trustworthy. Those are the solutions that can ignite exponen-tial growth.

III The Consumers' Call to Action: How Sustainability Is Shaping Consumer Behavior

6 How Sustainability Is Shaping Consumer Behavior

The new frame we want to establish starts with one question: What do consumers want?

Over the course of the past several decades, the advocates of the green mirage have hijacked that question, oversimplified its answers, and hammered them into the minds of business leaders. As mentioned in part I, they assert that the world comprises two groups: "sustainable consumers" and everyone else. Sustainable consumers—by definition the ones willing to pay a significant price premium for a sustainable solution—make up a small and commercially limited proportion of the overall market. This effect has become so ubiquitous and so numbing that the existence of a significant price premium is now the acid test for any sustainable solution, which makes the green mirage a convenient way for a business to dismiss ideas that focus on scale, volume, or alternative price positions.

Our plan in part III is to regain control of that question. The answer to "What do consumers want?" is multifaceted. It involves listening to their views, interpreting their actions, exploring their motivations and their barriers, and understanding their differences. A rich set of fresh answers to that question will help business leaders recognize the extent of pent-up consumer demand for sustainable solutions in their markets. Serving that pent-up demand creates vast commercial opportunities for companies willing to invest in bold moves and become first movers rather than followers. Instead of dismissing other strategies, they may need to go all-in on strategies built around scale, volume, and alternative price positions. These strategies will enable a company to move to the upper adoption curve in figure 2.1, the one the leads to exponential growth.

Part III dives deeper into the sources of that pent-up demand: what consumers want and how they are changing their behavior. We uncover the role sustainability plays relative to other purchasing criteria and how it shapes consumer needs and preferences. We highlight the primary adoption barriers—affordability, accessibility, product knowledge, and trust—that companies need to dissolve to make sustainable solutions grow at scale.

The Pace of Change Is Accelerating

Sustainability now holds a powerful position in the minds of the consumers. Their heightened awareness around sustainability has changed their day-to-day behavior, including how they make their buying decisions. Price, quality, and brand are product attributes that historically are known for affecting the perceived attractiveness of any solution in the eyes of consumers. The relative importance of these universal value drivers depends on the consumer and on the product or service they are buying. Consumers are driving the sustainability megatrend forward by changing what they consume, how they consume, and how they lead their day-to-day lives. We expect that the pace of these changes will continue to be measured in years, not decades.

In the core study we conducted in 2022, a total of 71 percent of respondents in North America and Europe said they have made modest or significant changes toward buying more environmentally sustainable products over the past five years. Some 56 percent of the consumers said environmental sustainability is more important today compared to last year when they make daily purchasing decisions. However, what is holding back the consumers from accelerating their commitment to making sustainable purchasing decisions is the existence of a set of barriers imposed and perpetuated by many companies. The most frequently cited barriers to buying sustainable goods and services are affordability (34 percent), accessibility (23 percent), knowledge (22 percent), and trust (16 percent).[1] Dissolving these barriers is the key for companies that want to unlock the commercial opportunities—growth, profit, consumer loyalty, and advocacy—that can come from bringing sustainable solutions to market. In reducing or dissolving these barriers, companies will accelerate growth by making it easier for even the most frustrated and mistrustful consumers to lead more sustainable lives.

There is no fixed sequence companies should follow to address these barriers. Some companies, for example, may not be able to address affordability in the short-term, neither through lowering their cost base nor through the commercial creativity that helps them implement different pricing structures and go-to-market strategies. But they can still address other barriers to improve their relationships with consumers. Our research shows that these barriers are interrelated, which means that dissolving one can weaken or eliminate others. Shoring up the knowledge about a product with credible information—both in depth and breadth—can also enhance trust, simply by shifting the ratio of positive to negative or dubious claims in the brand's favor. Knowledge can also change consumers' perceptions that they can't afford a sustainable solution because credible and trustworthy information can enhance their perceived value for that solution.

Removing the barrier of affordability can get more products in consumers' hands, which creates more positive user experiences and lays the groundwork for the loyalty and advocacy that consumers rely on when they seek out sustainable solutions, as we described in part I. The greater volumes also increase efficiencies and economies of scale, which can lower production costs and allow the company to make solutions even more affordable and accessible.

The Diversity and Power of Consumers

The stereotypical "sustainable consumer"—with an intense passion for all things sustainable and a high willingness to pay for sustainable goods and services across all categories—makes up only a small portion of the world's consumers. The belief that there is only one type of sustainable consumer represents an incomplete and inadequate view of who consumers are, what they want, and how they behave. Sustainability is now a present and influential factor in how *most* consumers make their lifestyle decisions and their purchase decisions. But the influence of sustainability on consumers is not uniform, neither in its intensity nor in its extent.

To understand these differences and make them actionable, we segmented consumers in North America and Europe by performing a cluster analysis based on two dimensions, using data from our two core studies:

- **Their commitment to sustainability.** Each consumer responded to a number of specific purchasing situations for 19 product categories.[2] For each category—for example, apparel—they ranked the importance of value drivers from a list we provided. The number and type of value drivers depended on the category but always included price, quality, brand, and environmental sustainability. The measure of an individual consumer's commitment to sustainability is the number of times that consumer ranked environmental sustainability among their top-five buying criteria across the categories they rated.

- **Their relative willingness to pay more.** We asked each consumer if they would be willing to pay less, the same, or more for a sustainable alternative within a certain product category. The measure of an individual's willingness to pay more for sustainable solutions is the number of times they stated that they would be willing to pay more across product categories.

Figure 6.1 shows the results of that analysis for European and North American consumers. Consumers fall into eight distinct archetypes, each with its own value drivers, attitudes, motivators, barriers, and information sources when it comes to purchasing sustainable goods and services.

While the core studies provided the structure for the segmentation, the basic interpretations and richer descriptions of each archetype

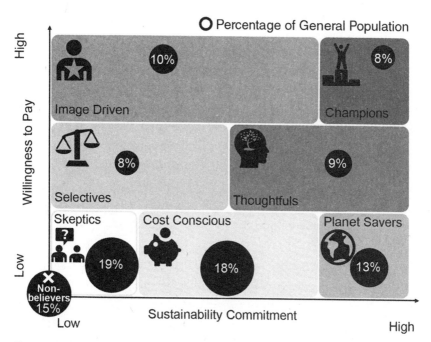

Figure 6.1

The consumer behavior map shows the eight consumer archetypes based on their commitment to sustainability and their willingness to pay a premium. The map also shows the percentage of the general population that each archetype represents.

derive from how the consumers responded to all the general and industry-specific questions in the large-scale surveys.

To test the segmentation and enrich the descriptions of each archetype, we conducted focus groups with more than 70 US consumers in March 2023 across seven out of the eight archetypes and then conducted one in-depth personal interview with a representative from each of the eight archetypes. The insights from the focus groups and interviews validated to a high degree the findings from our large-scale quantitative surveys, including

- primary motivating factors and barriers to consumers when it comes to purchasing sustainable products and services;
- the willingness to pay for sustainable product and service alternatives;

- the differences in their commitment to sustainability in terms of behavior in their everyday lives and their purchase decisions.

The consumers themselves brought the finer distinctions to life as they described their aspirations, their experiences, and their frustrations. The insights from the qualitative research also confirmed our hypotheses around consumer loyalty, advocacy, information search, and their thoughts on the ways for-profit companies, nongovernmental organizations, governments, and consumers themselves should address the challenges of environmental sustainability.

Meet the Consumers behind the Demand Revolution

Two extremes anchor the segmentation in figure 6.1. The *champions*, who represent 8 percent of the population, are fully committed to sustainability and are willing to pay premium prices to support that lifestyle. The *nonbelievers* (15 percent) never take sustainability into account in their buying decisions, nor do they have any intention of paying a premium for a sustainable solution.

Champions and nonbelievers are the two archetypes that underpin the green mirage. By conflating a commitment to sustainability with a willingness to pay more for it, the green mirage assumes that consumers have a binary "yes–no" relationship with sustainability: if you aren't all in, then by definition you are "all out." Yet our more detailed segmentation shows that the consumers who are either all-in or all-out comprise less than a quarter of the general population.

The demand revolution, although spearheaded by the champions, is also taking place across the remaining 77 percent of the population represented by the other six archetypes shown in figure 6.1. That is a relatively large number of segments, but this complete and nuanced breakdown is necessary to enable companies to find their own path to exponential growth with sustainable solutions. Designing and marketing a sustainable solution that will appeal to a combination of the champions, the *image driven*, and the *thoughtfuls* (27 percent of the population) will be much different from designing and marketing a solution to appeal to the *planet savers*, the *cost conscious*, and the thoughtfuls (40 percent of the population).

The dynamism and nuances of all the archetypes emerge when we look beyond aggregate averages and beyond common segmentation characteristics such as demographics. Our analysis of the demographics of each archetype shows no significant deviations. The demand revolution cuts across gender, income, geography, and generations with relatively equal force. Male baby boomers in the United States, for example, show a similar commitment to sustainability and the willingness to pay a premium as female millennials in Germany or France. Demographics therefore provide limited insights into whom a company should target with a sustainable solution.

The commercially relevant differences across the archetypes start to emerge when we look at the weight of consideration each archetype gives to purchase criteria such as price, quality, brand, and sustainability. Figure 6.2 shows the relative importance of these four value drivers by archetype, aggregated across the 19 product categories we tested. The aggregate score for sustainability aligns with the archetypes' position along the horizontal axis of the map shown in figure 6.1.

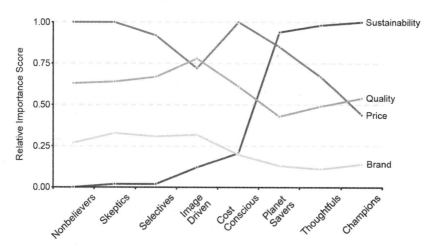

Figure 6.2

Aggregated view of the relative importance of sustainability, price, quality, and brand as value drivers across the eight consumer archetypes.

All of the segments make trade-offs in different ways across these four major value drivers. Sustainability and brand matter roughly equally for the cost conscious, who consider price to be their most important value driver or purchase criterion, but sustainability ranks as the primary value driver for the planet savers, thoughtfuls, and champions.

Disaggregating the information in figure 6.2 by category not only reveals more commercially relevant and actionable insights but also underscores how the green mirage can cripple a company's efforts to bring a sustainable product to market. Figure 6.3 shows the percentage of consumers by archetype who ranked sustainability among their top-five purchase criteria for the given category.

The importance of sustainability remains robust for the champions, thoughtfuls, and planet savers across all categories. The variation by category is wider for the cost conscious and the image driven, and the importance of sustainability is marginal in some categories for the *selectives* and *skeptics*. Within each archetype, sustainability tends to have its lowest priority in financial services and in leisure and travel. In financial services, evaluations often depend more on the way a service is delivered than on the nature of the intangible service itself, which makes the sustainability aspect harder to assess consistently at this point in our research. The relatively low emphasis that some archetypes place on sustainability in leisure and travel aligns with statements we heard during the focus groups. "If I'm taking vacation, that [sustainability] is the last thing I'm thinking about," said one selective. Another participant in the same group said, "If I'm on vacation, I feel like I've earned it."

To show the limitations of the green mirage and the importance of understanding the consumer perspective, let's now look at a potential product for the beauty and personal-care category, which is line 3 in figure 6.3. The implementation of a skimming strategy with a premium price position would exclude the planet savers and cost conscious archetypes from the potential market and presumably a significant portion of the thoughtfuls, for whom price is the second most important purchase criterion. The green mirage thus leaves the company with only the champions as a target market, although it may also attract

	Champions	Thoughtfuls	Planet Savers	Cost Conscious	Image Driven	Selectives	Skeptics
Energy							
1. Heating	99%	92%	97%	78%	46%	40%	49%
2. Electricity	98%	94%	97%	79%	47%	37%	44%
Consumer goods & retail							
3. Beauty & personal care	93%	86%	94%	71%	60%	39%	36%
4. Grocery & HH shopping	95%	88%	92%	71%	51%	36%	30%
5. Restaurants	92%	89%	90%	61%	50%	31%	29%
6. Electronics & HH appliances	97%	83%	93%	57%	42%	37%	24%
7. Furniture	96%	81%	90%	56%	44%	34%	22%
8. Apparel, fashion, & footwear	91%	81%	90%	47%	44%	28%	22%
Construction							
9. Home renovation	96%	83%	92%	45%	27%	12%	9%
Automotive							
10. Personal mobility	90%	79%	89%	45%	23%	15%	7%
11. On-demand private mobility	91%	77%	88%	43%	17%	14%	7%
Leisure, travel, & transportation							
12. Local public transportation	90%	80%	89%	45%	27%	14%	10%
13. Long-distance transportation	96%	81%	92%	36%	22%	14%	5%
14. Holiday packages	90%	77%	89%	32%	21%	10%	6%
15. Places to stay	89%	66%	82%	24%	18%	8%	3%
Financial services							
16. Personal financial investments	85%	75%	84%	41%	27%	12%	5%
17. Cryptocurrencies	89%	63%	79%	36%	26%	19%	10%
18. Personal borrowing	86%	66%	75%	30%	26%	18%	8%
19. Personal banking	87%	70%	73%	30%	18%	10%	6%

Figure 6.3

The share of consumers within each archetype that ranks sustainability as a top-five purchasing criteria across 19 product categories. The chart omits the non-believers because they do not rank sustainability as a top-five purchase criterion in any category. HH = household.

some image-driven consumers at the fringes because those consumers place relatively high importance on quality. That means the company has an addressable market of roughly 8–10 percent of the general population. It would also therefore assume that the remaining population's unwillingness to pay a premium means that those consumers—the vast majority—must have no interest in sustainability.

The consumers represented in figure 6.3 beg to differ. Sustainability is a top-five value driver for 94 percent of planet savers and earns a similarly strong score among the thoughtfuls (86 percent). Even 71 percent of the cost-conscious consumers rank sustainability as a top-five value driver in the beauty and personal-care category. The insistence on a skimming strategy with a premium-price position thus excludes 40 percent of the population with a strong interest in sustainability. In this example, these 40 percent would account for a significant portion of the market's pent-up demand, which will remain untapped until affordable, accessible, and trustworthy sustainable solutions hit the market. Those are the solutions that companies will not pursue as long as they buy into the green mirage.

Companies that believe in the demand revolution, however, have additional information they can draw on to close their perception gap and pursue exponential growth with sustainable solutions. We found that the eight archetypes share important characteristics that companies can incorporate into their commercial strategies:

- **A distaste for waste:** Even the skeptics and nonbelievers are keenly aware of the destructive power of certain consumer habits and corporate practices. They share an aversion to waste and inefficiency, although the archetypes vary considerably in the extent to which the awareness and aversion alter their day-to-day behavior. Nonetheless, the common thread is a baseline of common sense that seems to span all the archetypes. Companies should not underestimate the commonsense power and appeal of an antiwaste message.

- **A personalization of sustainability:** Many focus-group participants and interviewees linked sustainability to personal health and well-being and thus de-emphasized the overall social or environmental impact. They act as much in their own self-interest as for the benefit of others.

- **An appetite for more positive experiences:** The user experience is vitally important for consumers when they purchase and use sustainable solutions. A positive experience when using a product or service not only helps validate the claims the seller has made but also heightens their awareness and inspires them to look for solutions to other needs.

- **Critical thinking:** Every consumer has unresolved questions and lingering frustrations about their inability to find credible answers. The number of questions they have and the intensity of their frustrations vary by archetype, as the detailed stories in chapters 7, 8, and 9 show.

- **The power of personal and social networks:** As we mentioned in part I, one of the most profound findings of our core studies was the power of personal and social networks in influencing consumer opinions. While this influence took on different forms and intensities across the archetypes, it is one feature that all of the archetypes— even the nonbelievers—have in common.

- **Shared responsibility for sustainability goals:** Every archetype sees progress on sustainability as a shared responsibility of for-profit companies, nongovernmental organizations, governments, and consumers themselves. The archetypes do differ, however, in their views on the need for more governmental regulation and which of the parties listed should play the most prominent role.

The concept of "crossing the chasm" provides an appropriate way to view the differences between the green mirage and the demand revolution, drawing on the insights from the eight consumer archetypes. Introduced by Geoffrey Moore in the 1990s, the chasm is a "crack" in the adoption curve for high-tech products. It is the space that "separates the early adopters from the early majority. This is by far the most formidable and unforgiving transition in the Technology Adoption

Life Cycle, and it is all the more dangerous because it typically goes unrecognized."[3]

When the believers in the green mirage look across the chasm, they see only a mass of disingenuous consumers who claim to be interested in sustainable solutions but are steadfastly unwilling to pay for them. When the believers in the demand revolution look across the chasm, they see a large and differentiated market of consumers who are willing to change and ready to adopt as soon as they have affordable, accessible, trustworthy products. Their existence reduces or minimizes the chasm, accelerates adoption time, and creates the potential for first-mover advantages and long-term competitive advantages anchored in consumer stickiness, loyalty, and advocacy. The combination of archetypes that a company targets will depend on the company's objectives, innovation capabilities, and ability to balance commercial creativity with creative destruction.

That's why we will dive deeply into the eight archetypes in the next three chapters. Chapter 7 covers the two extremes, the champions and the nonbelievers. Chapter 8 covers the image driven, the planet savers, and the thoughtfuls because these segments have either a strong affinity for sustainability or a specific perspective on it. Chapter 9 shows the three segments who still make the most traditional trade-offs across price and quality in their day-to-day lives: the cost conscious, the selectives, and the skeptics.

7   Meet the Champions and the Nonbelievers

Champions and nonbelievers are at the opposite ends of the spectrum of sustainable behaviors in terms of intention, action, commitment. The starkest contrast between these two archetypes is how each prioritizes sustainability as a value driver along with other drivers such as price, quality, and brand. Champions rank sustainability among their most important purchase criteria in all 19 product categories we tested. The nonbelievers do not rank sustainability among their top-five purchase criteria in any category.

Consumers are far more differentiated than these two stereotypical consumers indicate, but the latter can still play a role in how companies implement the strategic frameworks we present in part IV. This chapter explores these two archetypes in detail, starting with the champions. We have grouped the two together because they represent the classical segments in the binary view of "sustainable consumers."

Who Are the Champions?

The champions, making up 8 percent of consumers (figure 6.1) live up to their name. Sustainability is their top value driver when making any purchase, and they are always willing to pay a premium for it if necessary and to the extent that their budget allows. They have made significant or extreme changes to their purchasing behavior and choices toward buying more environmentally sustainable products and services over the past five years. Some have made sustainability their way of life.

The strength of their motivations—relative to the overall sample—reflects their commitment to sustainability. Their sense of responsibility, fear of environmental damage, and desire to act in ways that will benefit younger generations are between 15–27 percentage points greater than the sample average.

Figure 7.1 provides an overview of the value drivers, willingness to pay, behavioral changes, motivators, barriers, and research habits of champions.

How to Win Over the Champions

Champions are always on the lookout for more sustainable solutions. Accessibility is a key barrier because in some instances they are not satisfied with the products and services currently available. They set a high bar that keeps moving upward. The limited availability of better solutions is the primary limitation on their ability to live an even more sustainable lifestyle, which implies a risk for companies that are playing the waiting game, one of the failure modes we described in part I. The champions are not necessarily concerned with brand names, meaning their switching barriers are generally low if another company does a better job of fulfilling their sustainability requirements. Champions are, as such, highly susceptible to the appeals of disruptive, sustainable natives who enter the market and fill the gaps that incumbents have been too slow to address.

Figure 7.1
The role that sustainability plays in the lives of champions. The higher the value-driver score (*top of figure*), the more important the driver is when consumers in this archetype make purchase decisions. The score reflects where each criterion (value driver) ranks among the archetype's top-five purchasing criteria. We examined an extended array of value drivers, depending on the specific product category, so the total scores for the four factors don't match up exactly across the different archetypes. The percentage points for barriers (*bottom of figure*) do not necessarily balance out because we also conducted testing with an "other" option, whose results have not been incorporated into this figure.

Importance of value drivers (score 0–100)

 **100**
Sustainability

 44
Price

54
Quality

14
Brand

Willingness to pay more

 In more than **9/10** product categories on average, the archetype is willing to pay more for the sustainable alternative.

Change in purchasing behavior over 5 years

5%	6%	24%	48%	17%
None	Minor	Modest	Significant	Extreme

Motivators

78%
A sense of responsibility

74%
A fear of environmental damage

64%
The benefit of younger generations

31%
A desire to act as a role model

48%
Feeling good about my purchase

8%
Social pressure

9%
Social recognition

Barriers

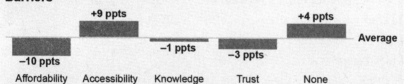

+9 ppts

+4 ppts

Average

−1 ppts

−3 ppts

−10 ppts

| Affordability | Accessibility | Knowledge | Trust | None |

Research before a sustainable purchase

 8%
I never research

51%
I sometimes research

41%
I always research

Champions have several strong motivations behind their actions, which means that a wide range of communication messages could appeal to them as they do their homework. For them, sustainability is more than the message. They spend an extensive amount of time on research before committing to a sustainable purchase. "I was vegetarian for a long time," one focus-group participant said. "But I recently switched to eating fish and poultry because I read that sustainably raised chicken actually has a lower carbon footprint than some meat substitutes." When champions do have a positive experience, they are highly likely to serve as advocates, at least until an even more sustainable alternative comes to market.

Champions are critical seekers of more information. A majority (57 percent) have some mistrust for the brands they typically use because they do not believe that brands are backing up their sustainable claims with actions. Some 83 percent of champions would probably not buy a particular brand again if they learned that the brand's manufacturer was not living up to its stated claims. Because of their heightened sensitivity to greenwashing, some 91 percent of champions research the sustainability practices of the brands that they shop for. Although they put in the effort, they often struggle to find the right parameters to make their judgments in part because there is a lack of a common language around what a "sustainable practice" really is.

Meet Tanya

"I think right now the way that I'm mainly sustainable is as much as I can buy a sustainable option, and if I can't afford it, I won't," Tanya told us as she shared her views on sustainability and how it affects her life. She added that she hopes that her "carbon footprint is better than others."

Tanya is 27 years old, and she lives in a major US city. She holds a bachelor's degree in critical race theory and English and a master's degree in poetry. Her passion about sustainability does not mean that she consumes less but rather that she does the best she can within her income constraints. "I'm quite frugal and quite resourceful," she said.

"I'm probably not, like, the biggest consumer." Nonetheless, her aspiration to live sustainably remains. When she finds the right solution, she said she "would spend the extra dollar on it."

"I don't know if they go hand in hand, saving the earth and saving money," one of the other champions in Tanya's focus group said. To some extent, they seem convinced that their money is needed to back up their words: "I think a lot of it is just putting your money where your mouth is."

Tanya grew up with a general level of awareness about sustainability, and that awareness increased and broadened as she grew older. "On the most basic level, I grew up with appreciation for the natural world," she explained. "There are cleanup efforts, and you try not to litter and things like that." When she went to college, however, her views of sustainability became politicized. "I began to understand there's kind of like this fledgling field of environmental justice," she said. "I learned a lot about people's efforts towards environmentalism. It's a conversation in my family a lot because I have a brother who's a vegan; he's very anticonsumerism."

What Motivates the Champions

Tanya links sustainability to her core values, a typical trait of a champion. One of the other champions in Tanya's group elaborated on this feeling: "I feel like it is philosophical; it has to do with my values. And more just a feeling taking an action that's in solidarity with the earth. . . . You would not like to cross a picket line by doing something that, you know, is like terrible for the environment."

Tanya worries about the labor conditions in the fast-fashion industry, for example, and that the fashion products end up in landfills when people don't want them anymore. "I definitely have that weighing heavily on my conscience a lot," she said.

The Barriers That Champions Face

Some 7 percent of champions claim they have no barriers whatsoever—neither accessibility nor price nor trust and knowledge—to living a sustainable lifestyle. For the remainder of the champions, however, having access to sustainable products is a much more significant barrier than affordability. The lack of access to sustainable products frustrates them in their desire to make the right decisions: "Mostly, I just want get to the end of my life and on my deathbed, no matter what the heck happens with the planet, [and] I want be able to look back and say, 'I did what I could.'"

How Champions Search for Sustainable Solutions

Tanya not only looks at companies' labor practices but also wants to know how much plastic is used in the manufacturing, shipment, and marketing of the products she buys. She also feels that "the system of designation of organic products and farming is also itself not perfect. So I think that's also a flawed metric." Another focus-group participant mentioned that they "do not only want companies to communicate and create more awareness but third parties validating it."

Tanya has a variety of information sources, but her primary ones are friends and family, followed by a small number of conventional or social media sources. She feels she has no single objective source of truth. She said she subscribes to and reads the *New York Times* and will sometimes go onto Wire Cutter, the section of the *New York Times* that compares products.

Who Are the Nonbelievers?

Nonbelievers are at the other extreme, constituting 15 percent of consumers (figure 6.1). They are never willing to pay more for sustainable goods and services, nor do they view sustainability as an influential or important purchasing criterion in any purchasing situation. They do not rank sustainability among the top-five purchase criteria in any of the 19 categories we tested.

Price is by far their most important value driver, while their desire for quality ranks above the sample average. In stark contrast to the champions, sustainability has not affected the nonbelievers' purchasing behavior over the past five years, which span the pre- and postpandemic periods.

Figure 7.2 offers an overview of the value drivers, willingness to pay, behavioral changes, motivators, barriers, and research habits of nonbelievers.

How to Win Over the Nonbelievers

The nonbelievers are not oblivious to sustainability and its relevance. The motivators shown in figure 7.2 indicate that many of them are aware of the potential effects of climate change and that many feel a sense of responsibility to act more sustainably. They are even aware of the availability of sustainable solutions and how much they cost.

A primary difference between nonbelievers and the other seven archetypes is sense of urgency. Nonbelievers have none. Even when they do research into sustainable solutions, they do not come up with a need or rationale that compels them to purchase a sustainable solution. Figure 7.2 shows, however, that they do have motivations that could lead them to purchase sustainable solutions. More than a quarter of them have a fear of environmental damage, and nearly half of them feel a sense of responsibility to behave in a sustainable manner. Yet sustainability never ranks among their top-five value drivers when they buy something.

Despite their disregard of sustainability in their purchasing behavior, some nonbelievers share the distaste for waste that characterizes a large majority of our focus-group participants and interviewees. They are tired of waste piling up in their homes. This antiwaste attitude is one potential path to reach the nonbelievers, try to spark a sense of urgency in them, and create an initial positive experience with a sustainable solution. A solution that is focused on reducing or eliminating waste and is combined with a compelling message and an affordable price has the potential to cross over and attract nonbelievers as well.

Meet Matthew

"I've been hearing it for decades about how we're all going to die," Matthew said. "And the hype, maybe it's trying to motivate people to

Importance of value drivers (score 0–100)

0	100	63	27
Sustainability	Price	Quality	Brand

Willingness to pay more

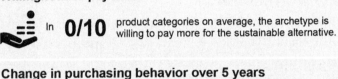

In **0/10** product categories on average, the archetype is willing to pay more for the sustainable alternative.

Change in purchasing behavior over 5 years

26%	24%	37%	11%	2%
None	Minor	Modest	Significant	Extreme

Motivators

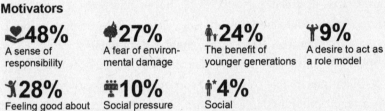

48% A sense of responsibility

27% A fear of environmental damage

24% The benefit of younger generations

9% A desire to act as a role model

28% Feeling good about my purchase

10% Social pressure

4% Social recognition

Barriers

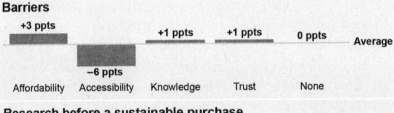

+3 ppts | −6 ppts | +1 ppts | +1 ppts | 0 ppts | Average

Affordability | Accessibility | Knowledge | Trust | None

Research before a sustainable purchase

46%	47%	7%
I never research	I sometimes research	I always research

be better and to behave better, but the hype kind of has the opposite effect. Why would I believe the hype today when I heard the hype 30 years ago, and it doesn't happen? What's the story? What are the facts?"

Matthew is 56 years old and lives on the far outskirts of a major US city. He holds a bachelor's degree in electrical engineering, and today he works with website creation and internet consulting. As a consumer, he describes himself as "cautious" and "very conscious of price and quality." But that doesn't mean Matthew ignores the topic of sustainability. The fact that sustainability advocates tend to "cry wolf," however, has sharpened his critical thinking. "I pay attention to some of it," he said, admitting that some of the information he reads is indeed compelling. "But then I have questions," he added. "I'm reading between the lines, and there's gaps, and there's pieces missing."

What Sustainability Means to a Nonbeliever

Nonbelievers are not directly motivated by sustainability, but that doesn't mean they are immune to or inert in response to its influence. Matthew takes a more holistic view of what sustainability means, one that doesn't necessarily correspond to more popular or emerging views. "I'm not in agreement with the political angle of sustainability," he explained. "I don't necessarily agree with a lot of the ideology, but I'm not wasteful. I do conserve."

Figure 7.2
The role that sustainability plays in the lives of nonbelievers. The higher the value-driver score (*top of figure*), the more important the driver is when consumers in this archetype make purchase decisions. The score reflects where each criterion (value driver) ranks among this archetype's top-five purchasing criteria. We examined an extended array of value drivers, depending on the specific product category, so the total scores for the four factors don't match up exactly across the different archetypes. The percentage points for barriers (*bottom of figure*) do not necessarily balance out because we also conducted testing with an "other" option, whose results have not been incorporated into this figure.

He notices tangible actions that companies undertake, but those efforts usually aren't strong enough to influence his buying decisions. "If a company says for every ten refrigerators we sell, we're planting a tree, that's something," he said. "But I don't necessarily think that if I've narrowed my preferences of a refrigerator down to two major brands and one's more sustainable than the other, I honestly do not believe that's going to influence me." He would give greater weight to the aspects that would have a greater day-to-day impact, such as "the features, the reliability, the customer service."

Matthew is no stranger to the themes and aspirations around sustainability. The spark for him to explore the topic was the documentary *An Inconvenient Truth* (2006). "Probably 15 years ago I was interested in everything that had to do with it, and I read everything I could read about it," he said. "I was probably more open and optimistic towards it when I was young because you want these things to work and you think these things will work." But he has drifted away from the topic over the years. The film raised many questions for Matthew that remain unresolved, but he has the impression that for too many other people it settled questions rather than raised them. He has become more cynical over the years, something he attributes to heightened critical thinking.

The Barriers That Nonbelievers Face

One of the biggest barriers—beyond the ones measured in our surveys—is criticism. "I don't want to argue the political aspect," Matthew said. "I want to argue the technical aspect of it. And so when [people] start arguing the political aspect of it, you're done." Matthew feels that people make a rush to judgment and pigeonhole him as a "denier" or as someone who is "just antiscience, or I don't know what I'm talking about, or I'm ignorant or whatever."

His questions about the sustainability of EVs are one example. "You don't need gasoline. Well, that sounds great," he explained. "Well, stop and think. First off, where's all the electricity coming from to recharge that car? The amount of energy to get from point A to point B, whether it's coming out of gasoline and refined, or whether it's coming from electricity, it's the same energy, the same amount of energy." The batteries are another issue. Matthew wonders about "the metals that need to be mined, the amount of energy that goes into mining those metals to make those batteries." He wonders why asking such questions is not considered to be a legitimate or favorable view of sustainability. He feels the reason is that "it contradicts the immediate, popular, politically motivated view of sustainability." He continued, "Those are issues that people don't think about. What good is it right now versus where did it come from originally? What did it cost to engineer, mine, and manufacture, and what is it going to cost to dispose of or recycle in the future?" Finally, price becomes a consideration. "As a consumer myself, do I want a really expensive car, [and] in four or five years I have to make a huge investment into it to replace that battery pack? I don't want that," he said.

Shifting to sustainable solutions in general, Matthew noted that "often sustainable product alternatives come at a premium because they for some reason require additional procedures in the production and therefore come at a higher cost." He added that these green premiums are "absolutely a barrier for me. I'm price conscious, and I believe that certain things are going to cost more because of that, and I'm not willing to pay for that."

How Nonbelievers Search for Sustainable Solutions

Within all archetypes, friends and family exert a strong mutual influence, perhaps the strongest influence in addition to social media and selected media sources. This holds true for Matthew, who discusses and debates the merits of products and services with his close friends. "I don't need to be on top of everything," Matthew said. "I do like technology, but with technology comes a lot of extra work." He singled out home automation as an example of a current trend and said that "most people I know don't mess around with home automation because of the amount of extra research and time and effort it goes into."

When making a purchase, Matthew said he will "do a lot of online research, and I take into consideration the size of the item, the shipping, the shipping cost. If something goes wrong, how much of a hassle would it be to return it, how much would that cost me in time and money?" The research he does enhances rather than diminishes his doubts about the sustainability claims that companies make. "It makes no difference to me whatsoever because whatever that company is doing, I don't believe that it's having the impact that is intended," he explained. "They are doing it to appease the public, or they're doing it to appease a group or whatever to say, hey, we're a sustainable company." He added, "The reasons people believe these things varies, so everyone needs to really develop critical thinking skills. When you read something, just don't take it for granted as fact. Dig into it a little bit. What are the facts? What facts are missing?" He admitted, "I don't have the answers. I'm not a scientist, but I know what my questions are."

8 Meet the Image Driven, the Planet Savers, and the Thoughtfuls

Between the extremes of the champions and the nonbelievers are six other archetypes whose purchase decisions involve complex trade-offs among sustainability, price, quality, brand, and other category-specific factors. In this chapter, we explore the three archetypes that share a trait with the champions, as shown in figure 6.1. The image driven show a relatively frequent willingness to pay more for sustainable solutions, whereas the thoughtfuls and the planet savers exhibit a high commitment to sustainability. These three archetypes make up roughly one-third of consumers.

Who Are the Image Driven?

The image driven, who represent 10 percent of the general population (figure 6.1), are highly aware of their personal image. They aspire to live sustainably, are usually willing to pay more for sustainable solutions, and claim that they have made major changes in their buying behavior toward being more sustainable.

At the same time, they exhibit a complex duality. Although they desire social recognition, feel social pressure, and want to act as role models, their emphasis on image does not always lead them to prioritize sustainability when they make purchase decisions. As figure 6.3 shows, they tend to give greater weight to sustainability in categories that affect their outward image or the perception of themselves, such as beauty and personal care.

Image-driven consumers stay on top of trends. They find new, fashionable, and tech-savvy offerings attractive, especially if they come from a trusted brand. But they are also the most distrustful archetype because any solution socially perceived as wrong or inappropriate can disproportionately affect their personal image. They do their homework to combat greenwashing. Figure 8.1 provides an overview of the value drivers, willingness to pay, behavioral changes, motivators, barriers, and research habits of the image driven.

How to Win Over the Image Driven

To win over the image driven, companies need to convince them that they have *the right* sustainable solution. For the image driven, the biggest barrier to living more sustainably is finding what they want. More often than any other archetype, they cite accessibility as a barrier. What they want is more than the presence of a sustainable feature. The approach "if it's green, it's good enough" will not appeal to them. What wins them over is a message that says "greener and . . ."; they want the best solution to a specific underlying need and are willing to pay a premium for preferred brands. The image driven have the highest score for quality among all the archetypes, and they are the least price-sensitive consumers except for the thoughtfuls and champions. The score for brand shown in figure 8.1 may seem low relative to price and quality,

---

→

Figure 8.1
The role that sustainability plays in the lives of the image driven. The higher the value-driver score (*top of figure*), the more important the driver is when consumers in this archetype make purchase decisions. The score reflects where each criterion (value driver) ranks among the archetype's top-five purchasing criteria. We examined an extended array of value drivers, depending on the specific product category, so the total scores for the four factors don't match up exactly across the different archetypes. The percentage points for barriers (*bottom of figure*) do not necessarily balance out because we also conducted testing with an "other" option, whose results have not been incorporated into this figure.

Importance of value drivers (score 0–100)

12 Sustainability   **72** Price   **78** Quality   **32** Brand

Willingness to pay more

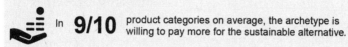

In **9/10** product categories on average, the archetype is willing to pay more for the sustainable alternative.

Change in purchasing behavior over 5 years

5%	13%	33%	36%	13%
None	Minor	Modest	Significant	Extreme

Motivators

66% A sense of responsibility

51% A fear of environmental damage

47% The benefit of younger generations

25% A desire to act as a role model

45% Feeling good about my purchase

13% Social pressure

15% Social recognition

Barriers

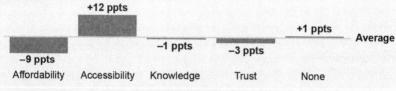

+12 ppts

+1 ppts   Average

−1 ppts   −3 ppts

−9 ppts

Affordability   Accessibility   Knowledge   Trust   None

Research before a sustainable purchase

12% I never research   **41%** I sometimes research   **47%** I always research

but it is nonetheless the second-highest importance score across all eight archetypes. The image driven are the segment that is least likely to accept a quality penalty. They will spend considerable investments of time and money on research and in return expect high quality.

Some 47 percent of the image driven—or 28 percentage points higher than the sample average—always research the brands that they shop from to ensure that the brands' practices are sustainable. They also have a higher degree of mistrust when it comes to whether they trust brands they typically use to live up to their claims with actions. Some 64 percent of the image driven agree to some extent that brands typically do not back up their environmental claims with actions. That is 17 percentage points higher than the sample average.

If this segment makes up the majority of a company's target segment, the company could make skimming a potentially viable strategy. But we also see the image driven making up a target group that includes the selectives, the thoughtfuls, and the champions in a consumer-goods category. The right product or the right portfolio could address more than a quarter of the general population and even earn a slight premium as well.

Feeling good about their purchases and achieving social recognition are relatively strong motivators for the image driven, including Jennifer, with whom we spoke at length.

Meet Jennifer

"I definitely am a consumer!" Jennifer said. "I am always shopping. I'm always out looking at the newest things, [and] all my neighbors know I'm always buying new things." Jennifer is 56 years old and lives with her dog in a townhome in an urban area in the United States. When she makes her purchases, she always has a purpose in mind, and that purpose is not always something as grand as saving the world. "Functionality is very key," she said, noting that her buying criteria are usually "functionality and then longevity, then probably sustainability." She may consider a sustainable product, but "if it doesn't suit my purpose, I would probably go buy something else."

Jennifer's evolution as a consumer began with a distaste for waste, which has made her more conscious of the quality of what she buys and especially how long it will last. "Maybe ten years ago, I didn't care at all," she said. "I'd heard of sustainability and green buildings and all this. I just didn't pay that much attention." Nowadays her behavior has shifted. "I think I'm being more considerate about the longevity and what it would really mean to me if it helps save money and help save usage, things like that," she said. "I would never say I'm a tree hugger, but I want to make sure I'm just not wasting."

This sentiment has prompted Jennifer to undertake some steps that go against her passion as a high-frequency consumer and align more with sustainability. These behavioral changes include keeping lists of clothes she owns, something one of her friends inspired her to do. Jennifer is "definitely trying to cut down this year on my clothes consumption. I'm still buying new stuff, but keeping track of it, I think, has been an enormous help." She has also become "a little bit more creative with how I repurpose my clothes that I currently have."

She also stays on top of the latest technology trends, which often bring a mix of benefits, including sustainability. "I live in a townhome that I've owned for over 20 years that is always constantly a work in progress," she said, adding that she is "always trying to keep my home updated with the latest things." She was traveling on the day we spoke and said she had just used her phone to verify that she had turned off her air-conditioning at home. This is an example where the megatrends of digitalization and sustainability can reinforce each other, and we revisit such opportunities in part IV. "Just being able to have things like that, I think are really helpful," she said.

What Motivates the Image Driven

Social recognition plays an important role for the image driven, who also like to feel good about their purchases. Many, including Jennifer, look beyond themselves for motivation as well. Some 47 percent rate "for the benefit of younger generations" as a motivation, and 51 percent cite fear of environmental damage. Jennifer falls into both groups. "Sometimes

I look at [my sister's grandkids], and I just want to make sure that they have resources and pretty parks and can live on the river," Jennifer said. "This morning New York has the worst air pollution because of all those fires in Canada, and we have to be able to breathe air. So I just worry about making sure that they're not going to have to wear a mask, not because of COVID but because of just our earth and some of the damages that we're doing."[1] "I'm single, so I didn't really feel like I had that much of an impact," she said. "But over the last many years, especially significantly over the last three, maybe five years, I really started getting very concerned just because it adds up. I started to be really cautious."

How the Image Driven Search for Sustainable Solutions

Jennifer's months-long efforts to buy a new car illustrate how she searches for product information. "I'm doing so much research that it's driving me crazy because I still haven't bought a new car," she said. "But I just don't think I'm going to end up going the full way," she added, meaning that she probably won't get an EV. For one thing, she thinks that "sustainability for the battery cars is not really sustainable. Like, how many mines are they mining to get the battery? I mean, I don't know." She expects to remain loyal to the Volkswagen brand and buy a gasoline-powered car, though she admits that the allure of an EV is hard to resist.[2] "Several of my neighbors have bought the new Tesla, and we all go over and look at it," she said. "It's also more of a status symbol, like an image status symbol."

Jennifer shares the suspicions that many image-driven consumers have. "Well, I think you have to consider your source," she said. "I think you have to consider who's telling you your information because everyone's going to have a certain narrative that fits what they want." People have to make up their own minds; "I feel like people definitely skew things." Jennifer tends to rely on colleagues and friends and considers the interactions mutually beneficial. "I feel like I've shared a lot with what I'm doing with some of my colleagues and some of my neighbors. I talk a lot, so I share a lot of what I'm doing."

Who Are the Planet Savers?

The planet savers make up 13 percent of the North American and European consumers (figure 6.1). They are characterized by their strong commitment to making sustainable purchasing decisions, but they are not willing to pay a premium for it. The lack of willingness to pay a premium should not be interpreted as a lack of interest. Price is instead in general a key purchasing criterion for these consumers when making day-to-day purchasing decisions.

Their reluctance to pay more for sustainable solutions coincides with their high level of sophistication and maturity with respect to sustainability. For many planet savers, sustainability has already become a hygiene factor. One way or another—despite their financial limitations—they will find solutions because sustainability is a prerequisite.

They are more creative in how they resolve their trade-offs among sustainability, price, and quality. They do not feel it is necessary to "buy" a sustainable lifestyle when they can build one in other ways. A sustainable lifestyle is often not something new to these consumers. They are highly mature and knowledgeable about what it means to be sustainable and have been for years, which explains why we see relatively limited change in their behavior in the more recent past. They are motivated by a strong sense of responsibility, a fear of environmental damage, and a concern for future generations. It is in this segment that you will find many stereotypical "sustainable activists."

How to Win Over the Planet Savers

The planet savers, together with champions, make up the most mature and knowledgeable archetype when it comes to sustainability. They are drawn to companies and products that they *know* are more sustainable and are offered at affordable prices. But in the absence of an available or affordable solution, they are creative in finding ways to live a sustainable lifestyle. At the extreme, this can lead them to reduce consumption volumes or defer trying out new products.

Importance of value drivers (score 0–100)

94 Sustainability

85 Price

43 Quality

13 Brand

Willingness to pay more

 In less than **1/10** product categories on average, the archetype is willing to pay more for the sustainable alternative.

Change in purchasing behavior over 5 years

7%	14%	38%	31%	10%
None	Minor	Modest	Significant	Extreme

Motivators

 73% A sense of responsibility

58% A fear of environmental damage

49% The benefit of younger generations

20% A desire to act as a role model

 39% Feeling good about my purchase

6% Social pressure

6% Social recognition

Barriers

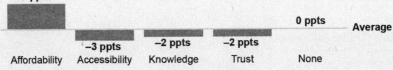

+7 ppts

0 ppts

Average

–3 ppts   –2 ppts   –2 ppts

Affordability   Accessibility   Knowledge   Trust   None

Research before a sustainable purchase

 19% I never research

 66% I sometimes research

 15% I always research

The planet savers are looking for inherently sustainable solutions when they decide to make a purchase. This creates an opportunity for companies operating along the consumer paths described in part I. In particular, "from volume to value" is relevant when this archetype is purchasing new products, where they look for quality products that last and have an overall higher lifetime value for the money spent. Also, planet savers live by the "from linear to circular" and "from excess waste to antiwaste" trends (figure 4.2). Secondhand offerings help them fulfill their commitment to sustainability but at more affordable price points. The planet savers are especially concerned with information that can lower their fear regarding environmental consequences. Highlighting CO_2 reductions in product messaging and showcasing minimum use of virgin materials, including "virgin" plastic, are particularly appealing to this archetype.

Affordability is the primary barrier for planet savers to live more sustainably. Some of the planet savers in our focus group are unwilling to pay more out of principle, whereas others, such as Lisa, face real financial constraints. In contrast to the image driven, planet savers would rather cut back on overall consumption to limit their footprint. Some of them will also make sacrifices on features such as design and convenience to follow a sustainable solution.

Figure 8.2
The role that sustainability plays in the lives of planet savers. The higher the value-driver score (*top of figure*), the more important the driver is when consumers in this archetype make purchase decisions. The score reflects where each criterion (value driver) ranks among the archetype's top-five purchasing criteria. We examined an extended array of value drivers, depending on the specific product category, so the total scores for the four factors don't match up exactly across the different archetypes. The percentage points for barriers (*bottom of figure*) do not necessarily balance out because we also conducted testing with an "other" option, whose results have not been incorporated into this chart.

Meet Lisa

"It just makes complete logical sense to take care of what you have," said Lisa, the planet saver we spoke with at length. "I don't understand why that's revolutionary." Lisa is 55 years old and a mother of three. She grew up in Iowa and now lives in an apartment with garden access in an urban area in the United States. She holds two university degrees, one in journalism and one in arts, and today she works as a self-employed author, writer, media consultant, and speaker.

"I come to sustainability based on the fact that I was raised with my grandmother, who was a Depression-era person," Lisa said. "So we never grew up with a sense of deprivation but rather creativity. I don't come to sustainability from the perspective of privation or scarcity mentality but rather respect for resources, making sure that we're using and having a joyful life."

What Motivates the Planet Savers

Although the initial motivation behind many of her choices is economic, Lisa does not feel as if she is missing out on anything as she conserves resources. She sees herself as a pragmatic consumer. In our talk, she is wearing a blazer from 1997 together with a blouse she bought at a thrift shop, and she still relies on her iPhone 8 because she does not want to contribute to e-waste. "I don't live like a monk," she said. "I have a wonderful life. I love riding my bike." That lifestyle extends to food as well. "I've got an herb garden. I've got my fresh mint going, I've got my basil, I've got my chives in the back and the front gardens. And so, again, I feel as if I don't eat like a monk. I had a great breakfast wrap."

"I don't like to put things in the waste stream, if possible," she said. For clothes, she has a "one-in, one-out policy," and the new article of clothing "has to match at least three or four things in my ensemble in my closet before I'll even buy it. So I really try to think about minimizing the impact that I have on my environment while still having what I would consider a comfortable life."

How Planet Savers Search for Sustainable Solutions

Planet savers are in general highly knowledgeable about what sustainability means. Like Ben, our representative for the thoughtful archetype, Lisa sees her research and her interactions with friends on social media as a two-way street. She is happy to share her experiences and creative sustainable behaviors with others—not to point a finger but to inspire and advocate. "My financial resilience isn't where it used to be, [so] I have to really think about what I purchase," she said. "What I do instead is if I know that there's something that is worth the price, and I either can't purchase it, or it's not something I need to purchase, I will tell other people about it. I'll use my social channel to say, 'Hey, do you know that they've got this product that does this and does that?' and then I use the appropriate hashtags to leave the digital breadcrumbs for the person for whom price is not an object."

She wishes that companies would also find a way to leave better digital breadcrumbs. The volume of available options, combined with the search costs for information, can quickly become so overwhelming that consumers end up sticking to their current brand not out of loyalty but simply by default because the cost to find an alternative is too high. "Most people look at the flanks of boxes of toothpaste in the store, and they're like, 'I don't know, I always buy this,' and it goes in [their basket]," she said. She thinks it could make a difference not only if someone knew more about product quality but also "if they could even see, oh, 'If I buy this, I'm helping them, and I'm also feeding a person, and I'm also doing this.'"

Lisa thinks that to effectively communicate the benefits of their products companies "just really have to be very explicit and almost pedantic when they talk with people about 'this is why you should buy what we're doing.' Even if it is something silly, just really put some personality into your brand that makes people remember. Use the carrot not the stick." She is hopeful about the effects from better communication: "You don't need to convince 100 percent of the people. You only need 33 percent of the people on board. So if we [companies] can even go to markets or demographics or communities where there's presumed resistance to your messaging and convert 33 percent of them, you can move the needle. So I would just encourage you to keep whittling away at that group instead of writing them off."

When consumers have their antennae up, they can discover affordable ways to make their lives more sustainable. Lisa illustrated this with a home-improvement example. When she moved into a house several years ago, "we installed the boiler that was the right size for the building" with the help of "tax credits and a rebate from our energy company." Her energy costs and bills plummeted as a result. "But the only reason we did that was because I knew that it was possible," Lisa said. "So I wish that there was a more concerted effort to let people know that there's a financial carrot, a financial benefit to doing the right thing. And if that means the energy company loses a certain amount of money for a specific quarter, I think our planet's worth it."

Planet savers are also active advocates for sustainable goods and services. When they make a recommendation, however, they prefer a positive and reinforcing approach rather than a high-pressure environmental pitch. "I won't say, 'If you don't buy this car, you're gonna go to hell, and you're ruining the planet and terrible for you,'" said one of our focus-group participants. "I'll just say, 'Man, this is freaking cool. You should try one. See what you think.'"

Who Are the Thoughtfuls?

The thoughtfuls make up 9 percent of North American and European consumers (figure 6.1). They share the champions' passion for sustainability and willingness to pay a premium for sustainable solutions, but to a lesser extent in both cases.

One of the six aspects that all archetypes share to some degree is an appetite for more positive experiences from consuming and using sustainable solutions. But for the thoughtfuls, that aspect serves as a guiding principle. Their relationship with sustainability is constantly evolving and deepening as they progressively discover new ways to weave sustainability into their lives.

Perhaps among all the archetypes, the thoughtfuls work the hardest to overcome the fact that most product categories lack a leader on sustainability in the same way that there are price, quality, and brand leaders. Using online research, social media, and information from friends and family, they cobble together their own short lists of innovative, sustainable companies. The reason why they are not willing to pay more for sustainable solutions across all product categories often traces back to their lack of exposure or awareness. If they cannot find a sustainable solution—or even conceive of one—it is hard for them to evaluate a price–value relationship unless they use another value driver, such as quality, as a proxy for sustainability.

Figure 8.3 provides an overview of the value drivers, willingness to pay, behavioral changes, motivators, barriers, and research habits of the thoughtfuls.

How to Win Over Thoughtfuls

Thoughtfuls make an interesting target archetype because of their position in figure 6.1. They share a border in the map with every archetype except the skeptics, which can make them a promising cornerstone for a company's efforts to find the largest possible target audience for a sustainable solution. To win these explorers of sustainable experiences, companies need to place communication at the center of their commercial strategy. Quantitative and objective information has the strongest appeal, so that the thoughtfuls can more effectively weigh their options in a purchasing situation. In return, thoughtfuls will reward these communication efforts not only with their purchases but also with their own dedicated advocacy.

The problem for many companies is striking the right tone and content in their communication efforts. Tighter regulations to fight greenwashing may prompt companies to make only rudimentary claims about sustainability in order to avoid the risk of legal action. Yet the tension between greenwashing and greenhushing creates another

Importance of value drivers (score 0–100)

98 Sustainability   **67** Price   **49** Quality   **11** ● Brand

Willingness to pay more

 In **5/10** product categories on average, the archetype is willing to pay more for the sustainable alternative.

Change in purchasing behavior over 5 years

4%	9%	33%	42%	12%
None	Minor	Modest	Significant	Extreme

Motivators

♥76% A sense of responsibility

♠62% A fear of environmental damage

54% The benefit of younger generations

⚥28% A desire to act as a role model

47% Feeling good about my purchase

9% Social pressure

11% Social recognition

Barriers

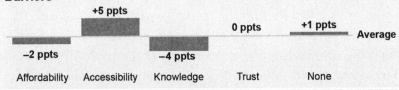

+5 ppts

0 ppts   +1 ppts   **Average**

–2 ppts   –4 ppts

Affordability   Accessibility   Knowledge   Trust   None

Research before a sustainable purchase

11% I never research   **63%** I sometimes research   **26%** I always research

high-reward opportunity for companies. In such an environment, companies can own the sustainability position in their category if they substantiate strong claims about how their solutions can help consumers fill a need more sustainably or lead a more sustainable lifestyle.

Companies should indulge the thoughtfuls' desire for constant learning and reinforcement. This is the archetype who will seek out and watch the infomercial about how a sustainable product is made or watch a story about the history of a brand from start to finish. Content marketing should be in focus to avoid simple appeals in the spirit of "it's only about the message," which will not resonate with them.

Likewise, "green is good enough" does not have a strong appeal to the thoughtfuls. They will make genuine trade-offs, including paying a higher price, if they find a solution that is overall superior and not only green. Getting to this conclusion means they have done extensive research to ensure that the products they buy are truly sustainable and worth the premium. That describes the current position that Ben, our representative for the thoughtfuls, ponders as he thinks about the furniture in his home.

Meet Ben

"I got my bed about seven years ago, and I wasn't thinking about sustainability," Ben said. "So I'm going to probably start looking at new products out there that could be sustainable." But the motivation is

---

Figure 8.3
The role that sustainability plays in the lives of the thoughtfuls. The higher the value-driver score (*top of figure*), the more important the driver is when consumers in this archetype make purchase decisions. The score reflects where each criterion (value driver) ranks among the archetype's top-five purchasing criteria. We examined an extended array of value drivers, depending on the specific product category, so the total scores for the four factors don't match up exactly across the different archetypes. The percentage points for barriers (*bottom of figure*) do not necessarily balance out because we also conducted testing with an "other" option, whose results have not been incorporated into this figure.

improvement and not merely to buy something sustainable, he said, adding that the new purchase may come when "we're looking to upgrade for our room."

Ben is 38 years old. He has a background in education and interpersonal communication and currently works for an information technology company. His wife is a teacher, and they share a house with their dog in a major metropolitan area.

Ben describes himself as a consumer who more often buys what he needs than what he wants. He looks for the quality of a brand more than the price of the individual product. He wants to know about not only the longevity of products but also what the brand stands for, what its mission is, and how it can improve his life. The sparks to his curiosity can come at the strangest times. "Last night I wanted to freeze something in the freezer in a Ziploc bag," Ben said. "And I was thinking to myself, I got all these plastic bags all labeled. There's got to be an alternative to it. That keeps me up at night because it's like 'plastic, plastic,' and we need to do more things biodegradable."

What Motivates Thoughtfuls

Ben's experience in purchasing an EV shows the importance of firsthand experience in changing someone's attitudes toward sustainability. When Ben bought his first EV in 2020, he did not make the purchase primarily for environmental reasons. "I don't like to purchase things that are just relatively inexpensive, cheap, because I'm getting a deal or if I'm getting a sale," Ben said. "You want to get something that's nice." That was a key motivation in his purchase of a Tesla. He considered Tesla to have the most rigorous testing and was drawn in by the technology. "That's a big passion of mine," he said. "I'm a big techie. I love having a whole smart home that's all interconnected and app based. That's huge for me." Buying the Tesla in 2020 has "made my life a lot easier in terms of traveling, going to places. I'm saving money, but also reducing my carbon emissions." He said that the purchase "was kind of the first major step I probably took. And since then, I really feel like in the last two and a half years, I've really made a lot of differences and a lot of changes in my life to actually better the planet and go more green."

Some of his other buying experiences indicate the struggles that the thoughtfuls have when they make trade-offs across sustainability, quality, price, and brand. He came across the shoe company TOMS on Instagram, and when he dug deeper, he learned about the company's commitment to sustainability.[3] The link between sustainability and shoes already existed in his family in part due to his wife's commitment to Rothy's, which are shoes made from recycled material and an example of a commitment to a circular economy.[4] When it came to the ultimate purchase decision, though, Ben remained loyal to Sperry boat shoes because "when you're loyal and true to a brand, it's really hard to give them up." Comfort and price played a role in the decision as well, but Ben also noted that "it's what my friends have. And I think sometimes it's all about fitting in." The sustainable product did not win in that case, but TOMS is at least now in Ben's evoked set of products.

How Thoughtfuls Search for Sustainable Solutions

Almost 90 percent of thoughtfuls do at least some research before making a sustainable purchase. For Ben, this research is part of an ongoing journey about learning what sustainable solutions are available. "One of my favorite quotes is 'The work you do is a reflection of yourself,'" he said. "I constantly want to keep looking out to see what other products are out there. I want to be completely in. And I just feel like there's more things I could do today that I'm not doing."

Ben's activity on Instagram led him to discover TOMS. He feels that interacting with social media and among friends and neighbors is a two-way street, meaning that he gets ideas but also wants to serve as an advocate. Some 76 percent of thoughtfuls cite a sense of responsibility as a strong motivation for living sustainably, a score that is second only to the champions' score in that category. Through social media, Ben learned about the local company Urban Canopy, which operates a composting service for a monthly fee. When a friend recently asked him about composting, Ben didn't hesitate to make his sales pitch. "I said, it's about like $16 a month. They take your bucket, then they replace the bucket, and then over time you start seeing that you could start growing soil," he explained. He has also told a friend about biodegradable dog-waste bags and soap bars without packaging. "I do want the people that do care to know that I could be a trusted adviser to help them out along the way," Ben said. He could "give them some bullet points or some good feedback to kind of what to look for, like what stores to shop at? Why sustainable is worth it in the long run? What's the OPEX [operating expense] and CAPEX [capital expenditure] savings in the long run?"

Ben did not grow up in a household where actions such as recycling were a priority, which has had some influence on his behavior as an adult. "You just start looking for other alternatives than what you grew up with because of how fast the road is changing," he said. "It's important to keep up with these trends. You don't want to lose focus because if you start losing focus, you start losing a little piece of yourself."

9 Meet the Cost Conscious, the Selectives, and the Skeptics

The three archetypes we explore in this chapter do not share an extreme position with the champions. They are not as strongly committed to sustainability, and only in a few cases are they willing to pay a premium for a sustainable solution.

The cost conscious, selectives, and skeptics make up roughly 45 percent of the consumer population. They include the most price-sensitive segments, although they still place high importance on quality. Sustainability is relatively unimportant in their mix of value drivers because they are not motivated as strongly by a sense of responsibility or a fear of environmental damage. They also tend to do less research than the other archetypes.

Who Are the Cost Conscious?

The cost conscious make up a significant share of consumers, 18 percent (figure 6.1). These consumers prioritize sustainability in certain product categories, but they are generally unwilling to pay more for it. In some ways they are similar to planet savers, but without the creativity because their commitment to sustainability is not as strong or pervasive.

Only about a quarter of the cost conscious have made significant or extreme changes to their lifestyles over the past five years to act more sustainably. Though sustainability plays a subordinate role in their purchasing decisions, they still draw motivation from a sense of responsibility and a fear of causing environmental damage. However, price is paramount in every decision they make, and product quality is significantly more important than either brand or sustainability.

Figure 9.1 provides an overview of the value drivers, willingness to pay, behavioral changes, motivators, barriers, and research habits of the cost conscious.

How to Win Over the Cost Conscious

To attract and retain cost-conscious consumers, companies need to design and communicate sustainable alternatives with a clear price–value relationship. They can use a wide range of tools from behavioral economics to increase perceived value of sustainable alternatives and thus accelerate their sales to the cost conscious. These tools include nudges, such as strategically placing a "decoy option" or taking advantage of "tendency toward the middle." Furthermore, price-design elements such as showing the "smallest number"—for example, going from annual to monthly subscription communication—can make the product seem less expensive and thus more appealing.

As with the planet savers, high-end brands should not necessarily disregard the cost conscious. This archetype's sheer size makes it interesting. There is instead an opportunity to reach these consumers via nontraditional channels such as the secondhand market, which is booming, and the appeal of the secondhand spans beyond affordability.

Figure 9.1
The role that sustainability plays in the lives of the cost conscious. The higher the value-driver score (*top of figure*), the more important the driver is when consumers in this archetype make purchase decisions. The score reflects where each criterion (value driver) ranks among the archetype's top-five purchasing criteria. We examined an extended array of value drivers, depending on the specific product category, so the total scores for the four factors don't match up exactly across the different archetypes. The percentage points for barriers (*bottom of figure*) do not necessarily balance out because we also conducted testing with an "other" option, whose results have not been incorporated into this figure.

Importance of value drivers (score 0–100)

21 Sustainability   **100** Price   **61** Quality   **20** Brand

Willingness to pay more

 In less than **1/10** product categories on average, the archetype is willing to pay more for the sustainable alternative.

Change in purchasing behavior over 5 years

9%	19%	46%	22%	4%
None	Minor	Modest	Significant	Extreme

Motivators

♥64% A sense of responsibility

🌱47% A fear of environmental damage

👨‍👧41% The benefit of younger generations

🏆18% A desire to act as a role model

35% Feeling good about my purchase

9% Social pressure

7% Social recognition

Barriers

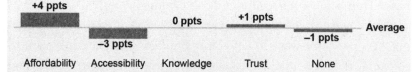

+4 ppts   0 ppts   +1 ppts   –1 ppts   Average

–3 ppts

Affordability   Accessibility   Knowledge   Trust   None

Research before a sustainable purchase

 24% I never research

65% I sometimes research

 11% I always research

Companies can take advantage of the emerging trend of buying second-hand to win over more price-sensitive consumers and thereby increase their market share. Circular business models such as recommerce, upcycling, and refurbishing can also appeal to this archetype.

Meet Charlotte

"Everyone would feel better if they could afford to make healthier choices for themselves and for the environment, but they're not given a lot of choices," said Charlotte, our representative for the cost conscious. Charlotte is 34 years old and lives with her boyfriend in a house they moved into a couple of years ago. She holds a college degree in theater and works as a freelancer in art fabrication. In terms of consumption, she describes herself as "frugal, minimalist, health conscious, and somewhat eco-conscious as far as affordability goes."

What Motivates the Cost Conscious

Charlotte's primary focus in terms of sustainability is her household's personal health. "Food and hygiene products are definitely the top eco-conscious ones, which also generally fall into more health conscious. But then when it comes to larger purchases like home-improvement costs or home-renovation costs or a car or travel, that's where it kind of has to stop because it becomes undoable budget-wise."

She is, however, passionate about food and to a lesser extent clothing. "People don't want to eat crap," she said. "People don't want to consume products that are bad. I think people want to make good choices, but we're often not given the option to make good choices, especially when a store only provides a bunch of junk that was not sourced ethically." Even food has recently become much more expensive, but Charlotte said that "we do what we can." Regarding clothes, she said, "I generally don't buy new except for when quality is really important for sustainability. So I've made an exception with shoes and coats because they're like something you'll have for multiple seasons. With the rest of my clothes, I generally thrift or buy used just because I prefer it, but also I appreciate the ethics behind it."

Charlotte and her boyfriend also take day-to-day actions in the spirit of sustainability, citing examples of things that "have been campaigned and drilled into the average daily consumer's head," taking reusable mugs to get coffee, not using straws, and not throwing away pizza boxes with food on them. "We're signing up for a composting program," she added. "And our city is notoriously really terrible about their recycling program. So like we recycle as much as we can."

The Barriers That the Cost Conscious Face

Price is the primary barrier for this segment, with 38 percent of the cost conscious stating that affordability is the main barrier to buying more sustainable goods and services. Accessibility was their second-highest barrier, at 18 percent. Charlotte agrees with both assessments, saying, "If I could, I'd probably go to Whole Foods all the time. But, yeah, it's about what's available where I am."

She also noted other barriers for herself, such as a lack of convenience and the challenges of living in an urban environment. She feels that her behavior may be changing for the worse because of these factors. "I'm from a different area of the country, where [sustainability] was in your nature, in your face more, and in your everyday life," she said. "Here there's only so much I can do that the city is supporting."

How the Cost Conscious Search for Sustainable Solutions

Some 76 percent of the cost conscious do some research into the sustainability practices of the brands they buy, while 24 percent generally take a brand's marketing at face value and do not conduct their own research.

Charlotte does her own research, but she appreciates why some people may come away overwhelmed or disappointed. "There's like a double-edged sword to how much the common consumer, even the informed consumer and concerned consumer, can educate themselves on," she explained. "When you educate yourself to a certain degree, you realize that it is kind of futile because the common consumer is prohibited from making the purchases that they'd like to purchase because of the cost."

She sees through marketing ploys, such as how companies "have a flower on it and have a very minimalist packaging" to attract a certain type of consumer, and she feels that the lower quality of information provided by companies leads to a degree of mistrust in their claims. This forces people to do more of their own independent research, but she feels overwhelmed with the information she finds. It helps to rule out some companies because of their practices. "But beyond that it's like you can't possibly research every single thing to buy ever," she said.

Social media and the internet help increase awareness about sustainability, and she feels that trend is beneficial. "We see the wildfires happening more and more affecting our air quality," she explained "It's starting to creep in. It's not just happening out there, it's happening here. I think it's in more people's spaces, and because of our accessibility to each other with the internet and seeing more people's personal stories on a daily basis outside of your own bubble, it makes the world smaller way faster."

Charlotte has a clear perspective on her own ability to change things. "As much as I'm passionate and care about it, I know that there's very little I can do on my own part, but it is like a moral conscience thing and also probably a principle thing," she said. She also doesn't look down on people who don't give sustainability much thought. "If you're in a position of power, you hold more responsibility," she explained. "But if you're just an average person, I appreciate that it might not be on your radar because maybe it's never been affordable to be on your radar. You have like a higher list of more important needs in your immediate life."

Charlotte is realistic that the ultimate course of sustainability will come down to money unless there is more government regulation. "Companies are never going to make a choice that isn't profitable unless they're forced to," she said. "So, yeah, I think that governmentally tighter standards need to be enforced in the US, so that the options that consumers are being given are more sustainable across the board."

Who Are the Selectives?

The selectives make up 8 percent of consumers (figure 6.1). They know about climate issues and their consequences, but this awareness rarely translates into sustainable purchasing behavior. Around a third of them state they have made significant or extreme moves toward acting more sustainably. However, they still prioritize sustainability only in a small, select number of categories. In general, their commitment to sustainability diminishes when it requires significant effort or sacrifice. Their mix of motivators and value drivers resembles that of the cost conscious, except that they are slightly less focused on price overall. This is especially true when it comes to sustainable solutions, where they have a significantly higher willingness to pay.

Figure 9.2 provides an overview of the value drivers, willingness to pay, behavioral changes, motivators, barriers, and research habits of the selectives.

How to Win Over Selectives

Selectives are a wild card among the archetypes. In general, sustainability is a weaker value driver for them. They are aware of the issues and the stakes, but they have passive rather than active engagement. They can quickly develop a strong interest or even a passion for sustainability in a particular category, however, if some form of extrinsic motivation changes their mind. That can happen if they become aware of a company offering clearly superior (sustainable) solutions because both quality and brand are relatively strong value drivers for them. They look for 'sustainable and . . .' products because the mere presence of sustainability is not enough to lure them to make a switch.

Other triggers can be strong advocacy through friends, neighbors, or social media or a visceral firsthand experience that makes environmental sustainability top of mind for them. Both types of influence show the importance of nontraditional outreach to potential consumers: the selectives do not seem to be responsive to the white noise of traditional advertising.

Importance of value drivers (score 0–100)

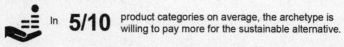

2 • Sustainability   **92** Price   **67** Quality   **31** Brand

Willingness to pay more

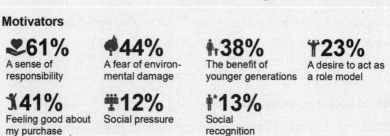

In **5/10** product categories on average, the archetype is willing to pay more for the sustainable alternative.

Change in purchasing behavior over 5 years

6%	20%	40%	27%	7%
None	Minor	Modest	Significant	Extreme

Motivators

61% A sense of responsibility

44% A fear of environmental damage

38% The benefit of younger generations

23% A desire to act as a role model

41% Feeling good about my purchase

12% Social pressure

13% Social recognition

Barriers

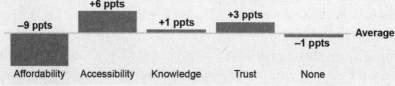

+6 ppts

−9 ppts

+1 ppts

+3 ppts

Average

−1 ppts

Affordability   Accessibility   Knowledge   Trust   None

Research before a sustainable purchase

15% I never research   **61%** I sometimes research   **24%** I always research

Meet Lucas

"Capitalism has done a wonderful job of bringing our entire species out of poverty for the most part, right?" he said. "But there are drawbacks to this, and one of those is the chase of profit at the expense of other things. And one of those things has been the environment for the last, I don't know, 200 years."

Lucas is 37 years old and lives in a suburban area in the United States with his pregnant wife and child. He holds a degree in journalism and works as a market research consultant. He thinks of himself as "probably your average upper-middle-class millennial consumer in the United States, which means I probably spend a little bit more money than I ought to be spending, and I'm pretty active in the economy. I think we spend money on something almost every single day. From a volume standpoint, we just buy a lot of stuff."

He is also aware of his tendencies as a consumer and the small role that sustainability plays in them. "I'm not saying it's majority, but there are people out there that make all of their decisions based off of sustainability choices," he said. "I'm just not that person right now, to be fair. We are impacting sustainability initiatives in general, but it's not top of mind."

In the spirit of the archetype he represents, Lucas is focused on environmental sustainability only in his future decision to buy a car. "Once our neighbor in our old condo got a Tesla, I think we started thinking

---

Figure 9.2
The role that sustainability plays in the lives of the selectives. The higher the value-driver score (*top of figure*), the more important the driver is when consumers in this archetype make purchase decisions. The score reflects where each criterion (value driver) ranks among the archetype's top-five purchasing criteria. We examined an extended array of value drivers, depending on the specific product category, so the total scores for the four factors don't match up exactly across the different archetypes. The percentage points for barriers (*bottom of figure*) do not necessarily balance out because we also conducted testing with an "other" option, whose results have not been incorporated into this figure.

about getting an electric vehicle," he said. "So whether or not we go all the way and buy a full out plug-in electric vehicle, or we get something that's a plug-in hybrid or some kind of hybrid option, that's something where we're actively going to be thinking about the sustainability of it. I feel like that's the future, and I want to engage in that part of owning a car. If I'm given a choice, I will choose not to hurt the environment." The decision will still come down to other aspects, such as performance and the accessibility to charging stations on longer trips.

"I would say that sustainability is only a priority for the car," he said. "But the rest it's all passive engagement. It's not an active choice I'm making right now." His passive engagement, however, has similarities to the health-conscious aspects of sustainability that other archetypes have focused on. "We do a lot of shopping in a Whole Foods," Lucas said. "Part of that is convenience. It's two minutes from my house. But the other part of this is that I'm very conscious of the kinds of things that I'm putting into my body and my daughter's body."

But that passive engagement with sustainability goes only so far. "I just had a party for my daughter's second birthday, and I'm serving meat products to everybody because that's what people want right now," he said. "So there is going to have to be some sort of real change from a supply side and demand side that business is just going to have to start putting forward."

The Barriers That Selectives Face

Price is a slightly lower barrier for selectives than for some of the other archetypes, meaning there is potentially additional willingness to pay that companies can extract. Lucas is optimistic that sustainability will cross an inflection point and become an important driver of most people's behavior, but the movement will not start with him, especially if it means paying higher prices. "I still think right now in this country you have to pay, I don't know, call it a 10 percent to 15 percent, maybe even 20 percent, premium for something that's sustainable relative to what the other thing is," Lucas said. That premium will become reasonable only when "that math gets a little closer to the 5 [percent]." "We make good money, and I'm still telling you this, right? It has to get a little closer to like 5 percent," he reiterated, indicating that he and his family have the resources to pay higher prices but will not make the commitment in the name of sustainability. "I wish that conscious capitalism was part of the way we're thinking about these things," he said. "And once the country committed, once our economy commits to the planet instead of profit, that will happen anyways. I think some of this is already underway."

In Lucas's view, two factors may change people's behavior enough to reach that tipping point: social pressure and even more intense climate change. "If all of a sudden all the neighbors started only using the natural, organic pesticides in the neighborhood, then I'm like, 'Maybe we should be doing this too, let's contribute,'" he speculated. The social factor "is absolutely big. But that stuff isn't going to happen unless the rest of the economy starts to catch up."

As for climate change, Lucas does not live with his head buried in the sand. "The news is scary right now, right?" he said. "You can see things like increase of wildfires, right, like other natural disasters. I have this creeping sense that the planet is fighting back in some sort of way. And so, in whatever capacity I have, I would like to be part of this solution." However, despite Lucas's awareness, he is not ready to make that change yet. "If there was more of an impact of climate change at my place as opposed to on the news, I think I might think a little bit differently about this," he admitted. "We're in the midst of the worst drought that I possibly could remember in my community," he said. "This is fascinating to me, but, honestly, I think I would need to see if we all of a sudden started getting more impacts like this. On a really consistent basis, like where it's drastic. I think that would force myself in particular."

For now, though, Lucas feels that the only way to lead a truly sustainable life is to get off the grid. "If you're really committed to that principle, you can't engage with the economy," he said. "The incentives aren't set up to reward that kind of decision-making right now. You really have to disassociate yourself from the economy, writ large.

That is really the only way to live a sustainable life." That kind of sacrifice has no appeal to Lucas. "Life is a little short," he said.

Who Are the Skeptics?

Like the cost conscious, the skeptics make up a significant share of consumers, 19 percent (figure 6.1). This archetype draws its name not from skepticism about climate change and its impact but rather from an overall skepticism about two things: consumers' ability to make a difference and companies' ability to make credible and trustworthy claims about sustainability.

The skeptics are similar to the nonbelievers in many respects, including that a majority of them are unwilling to pay a premium for sustainability in any product category, and they rarely do research to validate sustainable claims. However, they do differ in a few important ways. They feel a greater sense of responsibility and a greater sense of fear of environmental damage. They are also almost twice as likely to have made significant or extreme changes to their behavior in favor of sustainability over the past five years. Like the selectives, they do have some areas in their lives where sustainability does matter in their purchase decisions.

Figure 9.3 provides an overview of the value drivers, willingness to pay, behavioral changes, motivators, barriers, and research habits of the skeptics.

---➤

Figure 9.3
The role that sustainability plays in the lives of the skeptics. The higher the value-driver score (*top of figure*), the more important the driver is when consumers in this archetype make purchase decisions. The score reflects where each criterion (value driver) ranks among the archetype's top-five purchasing criteria. We examined an extended array of value drivers, depending on the specific product category, so the total scores for the four factors don't match up exactly across the different archetypes. The percentage points for barriers (*bottom of figure*) do not necessarily balance out because we also conducted testing with an "other" option, whose results have not been incorporated into this figure.

Importance of value drivers (score 0–100)

2 Sustainability   **100** Price   **64** Quality   **33** Brand

Willingness to pay more

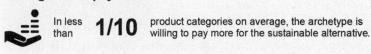

In less than **1/10** product categories on average, the archetype is willing to pay more for the sustainable alternative.

Change in purchasing behavior over 5 years

14%	24%	40%	17%	5%
None	Minor	Modest	Significant	Extreme

Motivators

♥56%
A sense of responsibility

🍃36%
A fear of environmental damage

👪34%
The benefit of younger generations

🧍13%
A desire to act as a role model

🧍34%
Feeling good about my purchase

🏆9%
Social pressure

👤8%
Social recognition

Barriers

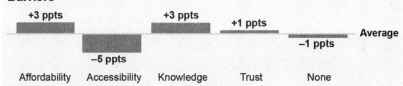

+3 ppts		+3 ppts	+1 ppts		Average
	−5 ppts			−1 ppts	
Affordability	Accessibility	Knowledge	Trust	None	

Research before a sustainable purchase

34%
I never research

58%
I sometimes research

8%
I always research

How to Win Over the Skeptics

To win over the skeptics, companies need to make sustainable solutions more attractive by linking sustainable features to other personal benefits. Skeptics are conservative not in the political sense but in the commercial sense. They recognize the issues related to sustainability, but they are often skeptical that their own actions will matter. They are reluctant to shift away from their conventional solutions unless they are presented with a better solution that has an overwhelming compelling argument behind it. They also mistrust claims of sustainability, although they rarely take it upon themselves to conduct research to investigate whether a product is in fact sustainable.

Crafting compelling arguments for skeptics is difficult. The communication strategy should focus less on piling on information about CO_2 emissions or other complex environmental elements and more on personal, tangible benefits that leave the skeptics better off. In the spirit of what Lisa, the planet saver, recommended, the communication should be "in your face" and even pedantic to drive home benefits in simple language.

The skeptics emphasize brand and quality in their purchase decisions almost as much as any other archetype, but they combine that emphasis with a relentless focus on price. This makes them far less likely not only to pay a premium for a sustainable solution but also to convert to new solutions. This tendency also makes them effectively immune to skimming strategies built around premium-price positions.

Meet Paul

"It's hard to believe what a big company is saying," said Paul, our representative for the skeptics. "It's wonderful if they say, 'We're sustainable,' but are you really, though? Or are you still dumping sludge into the Atlantic Ocean?"

Paul is 54 years old and lives in a rented apartment with his girlfriend. He holds a bachelor's degree in theater, and today he lives on the outskirts of a US metropolitan area and works at a live theater. He is passionate about challenging what companies claim. "It's great that you're a big company and you did this small thing to make it better for consumers and saying that it's healthy," he said, citing another way that companies say one thing and do another. "But are there 17 bigger things going on behind the curtain that are still being incredibly harmful?"

Paul describes himself as frugal. "I'm an organized consumer," he said. "I am very specific about our grocery lists and what we buy and trying to make sure that we aren't buying stuff we don't need." Underneath this skeptical and frugal exterior, however, Paul has tendencies that fit some of the broader definitions of sustainability: health, longevity, and less waste. One example involves pet-care products. "Sustainable kind of goes hand in hand with safer for us and our pets," he said. "I don't know if that's a correct assumption, but it's kind of how my brain thinks of it." So for cleaning products, he is more likely to spend a little bit more on sustainability.

For Paul, sustainability is also synonymous with something that lasts longer. When he wants to buy something, especially a durable good, he looks at price, ease of use, the brand reputation, and sustainability in his terms. "By that, I'm thinking I want it to last a good number of years," he said. He doesn't want to have to replace something every year.

Paul also has clear views about the need for recycling. "I think far too much stuff goes into the landfills," he said. "Far, far too much stuff goes into the ocean. My girlfriend and I are both animal lovers, and we hate stuff like seeing sea turtles trapped in six-pack can rings and stuff like that. All that stuff is bad, obviously." He said that he and his girlfriend try to do "whatever we can do to not participate in filling up the oceans with garbage and filling up landfills. I feel like it's not a lot that we can do, but we can do what we can do."

What Motivates the Skeptics

Paul feels that his behavior is changing in the direction of becoming more sustainable, but only in small steps. "I try to keep it focused on small accomplishments, small goals," he noted. "If I thought of what's happening in the world with pollution and everything else, it would drive me crazy and consume all my thoughts." In other words, sustainability is small scale and personal for Paul because he has no control over the bigger picture. "If you start thinking about, oh, are they recycling in Mumbai or in wherever, you can't do anything about that," he said. "So it's best not to get obsessed with it." He added, "It's easier for me to understand something if I'm thinking about it from more of a personal point of view as opposed to a more abstract point of view." What matters is "what I want out of it personally for me and the girlfriend and the cats and all the other pets around here."

The Barriers That Skeptics Face

Paul would welcome fewer inconsistencies and more convenience. "We go to the farmers' market every week, and my girlfriend gets these plastic tubs of cherries that she loves," Paul said. "But she gets them every week. So during farmers' market seasons, that'll be, I don't know, 24 of these plastic tubs, which is not ideal, but that's what she needs to make her healthy food. This unideal packaging is what we're going to have to deal with if we want to get these cherries that she likes."

Skeptics are extremely price sensitive, but Paul would still be willing to pay a marginal premium for sustainable alternatives if they remain within the affordability threshold. "I think if the cost of something is $10 more to be sustainable, that might be a little bit much for us," he said. "But if something's a dollar or two more, that's probably within our price range to be able to say, 'Oh, well, we can get this, and it's better, and we are only spending two more dollars than [if] we . . . get what we normally use, which is cheaper but not as sustainable."

How Skeptics Search for Sustainable Solutions

Only 8 percent of skeptics always research sustainable products, and 34 percent never do. Paul does his homework, but he feels that third-party or other forms of independent verification are important when he buys a product. If the product he's buying is a longer-term purchase, he will go online to see if the product and manufacturer "have good reviews from legitimate sites. When I've researched this stuff, it seems like there are sketchy sites where it's a sponsored thing, and it kind of looks like a company would kind of pay for good reviews. So I would want legitimate sites saying these are the pros and cons of this product."

If a company makes claims about sustainability and helping the planet, Paul will have his doubts unless he receives that outside validation. "If other outside sources—journalists, reviewers, people that look into this stuff and know what they're talking about—if they all say, 'Yeah, this company is actually doing this stuff,' that's what would need to happen for me. I want real experts."

He admitted that there are situations in which "I'm not going to be able to make an informed decision. I'm going to need somebody else to tell me, 'Yes, this is actually very good; you should use it.' To convince me, they have to convince more knowledgeable people about their products than me." His own recommendation for companies echoes Lisa's suggestion about the need for corporate communication that borders on pedantic. "Put labels on boxes and bottles and containers that are incredibly clear," Paul urged. "A big label on the front that says, 'No GMOs, no pesticides. Organic.'" He said the situation has improved over the past few years, but he still does not want to be forced to keep reading ingredient lists, "which is harder and harder as I get older and older and my eyes go."

The focus group we conducted also left an impression on Paul, indicating that exposure and awareness can help refocus someone's thinking. "Since we met in the group, I have been more aware of sustainability and what's good and what's bad," he said, again emphasizing small steps. "There haven't been earth-shattering purchases," he said. "It's like, 'Oh, should we buy these limes, or should we buy these organic limes? Well, let's get the organic limes.' But it has made a small difference in my life as well, and I'm assuming it made a small difference in everybody in the group's lives."

Paul will not give up his skepticism because he considers himself wired to be a "glass half empty" person. But he does have some optimism about the future course of sustainability. "I expect better communication [and] better labeling as the market dictates and more things become available," he said. "I would expect prices to come down a little bit as factories and plants and things improve in this area and because they're able to cut their costs. We're going to have more choices and slightly cheaper choices." He emphasized, "I think the more that it's talked about and the more that it's taken seriously, that's going to happen."

*   *   *

The wants, needs, behaviors, and attitudes of the eight archetypes also affect how they make purchase journeys as consumers. In the next chapter, we look at how the addition of sustainability as a powerful value driver—alongside price, quality, and brand—alters and augments the conventional consumer journey.

10 How Sustainability Changes the Consumer Journey

We expect the eight consumer archetypes will continue to exist regardless of how rapidly the demand revolution unfolds. But we expect each archetype's share of the population to shift over time. This will happen for two reasons.

First, sustainability will play a more prominent role in the purchase decisions of more consumers, which will shift the balance across sustainability, price, quality, and brand as consumers weigh their trade-offs. We expect sustainability to become a hygiene factor, which means that its presence in any solution is assumed. At that point, companies' ability to differentiate their sustainable solutions will take precedence.

Second, consumers will have a greater supply and variety of solutions as more companies make a dedicated effort to produce superior sustainable solutions at scale. As companies become more accustomed to the new innovation paradigm, markets will naturally shift away from having a small number of expensive solutions to a more differentiated or tiered state in which ranges of products better meet the needs of consumers and overcome the barriers they face. In markets where no company succeeds in achieving a first-mover advantage and the associated competitive advantages, we expect increases in both capacity and competition to put downward pressure on prices.

The Dynamics of the Eight Archetypes

The two extreme archetypes—the champion and the nonbeliever—have a small core whose views will probably remain unchanged. In the medium and long terms, we expect a migration upward and to the right across the consumer map shown in figure 6.1.

We recall here that the vertical axis of the map indicates the share of categories for which a consumer is willing to pay a premium for a sustainable solution. It offers no indication of the amount of such a premium. The horizontal axis of the map reflects a consumer's commitment to sustainability, as measured by the share of categories in which sustainability ranks among their top-five value drivers.

- **Upward movement:** Consumers will move up along the vertical axis, which indicates their willingness to pay a premium for a sustainable solution as more consumers find sustainability increasingly important and more industries offer accessible sustainable products and services at affordable prices. However, we expect this upward momentum to slow or stall in the long term as sustainability turns into a hygiene factor. The growth rate of the value pool for uniquely sustainable solutions will diminish as the market becomes so large that the mere presence of sustainability is no longer a differentiator. The volume of consumers willing to pay more will increase, but the absolute value of price premiums will decrease at a faster rate.

- **Rightward movement:** The strongest pull and fastest movement will occur along the horizontal axis as consumer awareness reinforces a commitment to sustainable living. But companies will impede this movement if their solutions still require significant sacrifices from consumers. Today, some consumers accept certain sacrifices, especially the planet savers. For such segments to grow, companies need to improve sustainable product options and break down the primary consumer barriers to adoption.

Rethinking What a Green Premium Really Means

We expect the willingness to pay a premium for sustainable solutions per se will decline over time and eventually disappear entirely in some sectors because sustainability will have become a prerequisite. To claim that a product is sustainable when consumers demand it anyway is not a point of differentiation and therefore does not warrant a premium. When every company has sustainable processes to produce, sell, and dispose of their sustainable goods and services, what matters is the *extent* or *degree* of sustainability. That is the form of differentiation that can justify a premium.

Put another way, the questions in the minds of consumers will no longer be the binary "Is your company green?" and "Is your solution green?" but rather "How green are you?" and "How green is your solution?" The answers to the latter two questions will be rich, differentiated, and multifaceted, not "yes" or "no." This shift will reduce the need for the word *green* because what matters to consumers is the manner in which a solution achieves a sustainable benefit, the extent of that benefit, how accessible and affordable it is, and how trustworthy the supplier is. In an effort to encourage the retirement of the binary meaning of the word *green*, we rarely use it in the remainder of the book except in connection with the green mirage or in terms such as *greenwashing*.

As the demand revolution intensifies, we expect the concentration of consumers in the thoughtful archetype to increase over the long term. They will have a higher level of commitment to sustainability, accompanied by a selective attitude toward paying a premium as they make balanced trade-offs across sustainability, price, quality, brand, and other product attributes. They will have a potentially high willingness to pay for solutions in some categories but no willingness to pay a premium in others.

In other words, the action will take place in the heart of the segmentation map, not at its extremes with the champions and the nonbelievers. Scale and speed come from the other six archetypes, supported and perhaps cross-subsidized by revenues from the champions, who may also serve as brand ambassadors. Selling more products to champions and dedicating development and communication resources to them will not yield a high return at scale because the segment is simply too small. Extracting more value from them means erecting more access and affordability barriers for the other segments, who compose the vast majority of consumers. If a company implements a differentiated pricing strategy, however, it may be able to tap into the champions' higher willingness to pay as a means to fund the company's efforts to scale.

However, an intense and narrow focus on champions that is designed to extract their relatively high willingness to pay may not be worth the risk of excluding the consumers in the other archetypes, who may not shop in the same channels as the champions or share their high commitment to all things sustainable or spend as liberally on sustainable solutions. Similarly, overinvesting in the nonbelievers will yield neither rapid nor significant change. It's hard to imagine a scenario in which they contribute to the rapid scaling that sustainable solutions require to ignite exponential growth.

Integrating the Segmentation into Existing Data

Many companies have already segmented their customers, either in general or with sustainability in mind. With respect to sustainability, A.P. Moller–Maersk has segmented its customers into leaders, implementers, explorers, and risk managers to better understand those customers' journeys.[1] In an interview with us, Leonhard Birnbaum, the CEO of E.ON, said his company has identified six customers segments, which the company also refers to as "archetypes."[2]

Most companies already know their own consumers in-depth or at least have rich sets of data about their purchase behavior. Their existing consumer insights and data and our in-depth description of each of the segments and their traits should allow them to make a useful allocation of their consumers to the eight archetypes we describe. Our objective with our sustainable segmentation model is not to compete or clash with existing corporate segmentations but rather to challenge them by showing companies ways to adapt or augment the segmentations they already have.

Some logical parallels exist between our sustainability archetypes and other classic archetypes. The stereotypical "price hunter" has links to the archetypes in the lower half of our model (e.g., the cost conscious and the planet savers), while quality-oriented segments may share traits with the image driven, thoughtfuls, and selectives. But these similarities are often superficial. To weave another segmentation into our eight archetypes, a company will need to look beyond basic dimensions such as demographics, purchase volumes, purchase frequency, geography, or other standard segmentation variables.

One goal in the defining of our eight archetypes is to inspire companies to look beyond conventional or partial approaches to segmentation and appreciate how multifaceted consumers are with respect to sustainability. As we have mentioned before, there is no such thing as a sustainable consumer.

Integrating the Segmentation with the Purchasing Journey

The next step is to integrate the segmentation into the company's existing purchasing journey. Figure 10.1 may conjure up a sense of déjà vu from a Marketing 101 class or a standard marketing book. We are not trying to reinvent the wheel in terms of marketing tools and concepts. We are showing how the wheel spins differently and faster for sustainable solutions once it's freed from the braking effect of the green mirage. In other words, our objective is not to teach anyone about what a sustainable purchasing journey is but rather to inspire business leaders to close their perception gap and get onto the right curve for exponential growth.

A focus on consumers alters the purchasing journey in ways that create strategic opportunities for companies to find and tap their pent-up demand, assume new leadership roles in their markets, and build a loyal base of consumers buying sustainable solutions. One of the biggest differences in the purchasing journey shown in figure 10.1 is the importance and power of the user experience and how it alters the value perception of consumers.

Figure 10.1 shows the purchasing journey of consumers when they buy sustainable solutions. Like the classic AIDA (awareness-interest-desire-action) marketing model, it shows how sustainability progresses

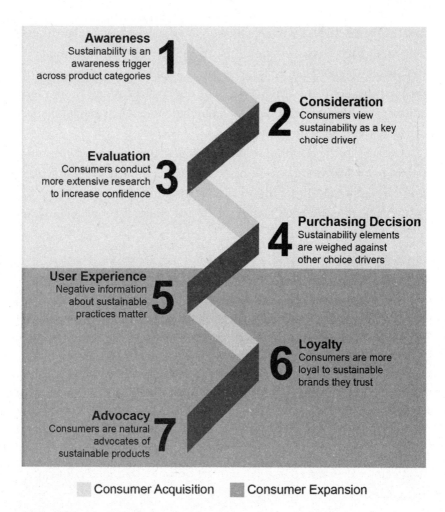

Consumer Acquisition   Consumer Expansion

Figure 10.1
The purchasing journey for consumers buying sustainable solutions.

from an aspiration to a commitment, then to a true driver of purchase behavior, and then to a driver of loyalty and advocacy.

Consumers behave differently when buying sustainable goods and services than they do when they make a traditional purchase. First, we extend the purchasing journey beyond the point of sale, which covers steps one through four in figure 10.1. This extended model incorporates opportunities for upselling and cross-selling mechanics to expand share of wallet as well as the power of advocacy to expand the customer base.

Awareness

We distinguish between two scenarios that create awareness. Needs-based awareness occurs when a consumer experiences a significant change, such as buying a house, having a child, or repairing damage from a natural disaster. Lisa (our planet saver) developed needs-based awareness when she replaced the boiler in her new house by taking advantage of government incentives. Want-based awareness occurs when a consumer becomes aware of a product or brand via advertisements, social media, or word of mouth. Ben (thoughtful) experienced that when he came across TOMS Shoes on Instagram, as did Jennifer (image driven) when she noticed that more of her neighbors were driving Teslas.

Companies have opportunities to create both kinds of awareness with attractive, credible, and meaningful sustainable claims. That is a challenge, however, because of the undercurrent of doubt and mistrust that pervades all of the consumer archetypes. A meaningful claim in that sense is one that has personal and practical relevance for the consumer. Based on our own observations as well as on what the focus group participants and interviewees described, we feel that companies continue to fall short on this challenge. Many claims or results about sustainability wind up in a corporate financial report or ESG document, which the average consumer will never read unless they are deep into research about a brand or product. Companies also craft such messages to have practical relevance for investors or regulators, not for the day-to-day lives of consumers.

The urgency to create awareness will become more acute as sustainability becomes an important purchase criterion for even more consumers. But it is only the first step in the process of creating a consumer who remains loyal and serves as an advocate.

Consideration

In the consideration phase, consumers determine the criteria they will use to make their purchase and come up with a long list of brands that could potentially satisfy their needs and preferences. Companies need to earn their way onto the list of potential brands when consumers take sustainability into account. As Charlotte (cost conscious) said, putting a flower on minimalist packaging is probably not enough to sway someone. Ben, for example, used criteria such as fit, comfort, brand, and sustainability to prepare his decision on which shoes to purchase. TOMS succeeded in joining his list of potential brands, alongside Rothy's and Sperry.

Positioning is more than staking a claim or even objectively being the best. As Al Ries and Jack Trout write in *Positioning: The Battle for Your Mind*, positioning is "an organized system for finding a window in the mind. It is based on the concept that communication can only take place at right time and under the right circumstances."[3] The goal is to occupy a space in the consumer's mind.

Let's use a thought experiment to look beyond shoes to other products consumers buy. If you plan to buy a car, and safety is your primary criterion, what brand comes to mind? If no brand comes to mind, you might turn to research and learn about Japanese OEMs such as Honda and Toyota.

Now let's change that primary criterion to sustainability. What products can you name that are synonymous with sustainability in any category, not just cars? If thinking as a consumer, you may have named Patagonia and Tesla. If thinking as an investor or as someone who follows business media, you may have named Unilever, though Unilever recently announced plans to pull back from an emphasis on purpose and, by extension, from sustainability. "In recent years, debate around brands' sustainability and purpose has arguably generated more heat than light," said Unilever CEO Hein Schumacher, who added that the company will no longer try to "force fit" purpose onto its brands.[4]

Positioning is hard to establish and hard to maintain but can bring significant long-term benefits if done well. As Ries and Trout point out, "IBM didn't invent the computer. Sperry-Rand did. But IBM was the first company to build a computer position in the mind of the prospect."[5]

Our most recent core study revealed that a large majority of North American and European consumers already rank sustainability as a top-five purchasing criteria in at least one product category. When we asked the focus-group participants to name a brand or product that is synonymous with sustainability, the champions could quickly come up with a few names, but the room remained silent when we asked archetypes such as the skeptics. In other words, a critical mass of consumers ranks sustainability as one of their most important purchase criteria, but the markets for sustainable solutions are still so underserved and underdeveloped that few consumers can name a brand that owns the sustainability positioning in a category.

When we introduced the perception gap in chapter 2, we noted the leadership vacuum in terms of sustainable positioning in many markets. If the pent-up demand is high and such a leadership vacuum exists, a company has better chances to capitalize on the demand revolution by "owning" that positioning. The urgency to do that in a market or category will become more acute as sustainability entrenches itself alongside price, quality, and brand as a primary purchase criterion for even more consumers. This trend is already well established for every consumer archetype except nonbelievers, skeptics, and selectives, but even selectives have at least one category in which they are willing to pay more for sustainability.

Evaluation

In the evaluation phase, consumers perform their detailed research, weigh their trade-offs, and narrow their list of potential options. As we mentioned, the research phase for sustainable goods and services tends to be longer and more involved than for nonsustainable goods in part because consumers struggle to find information that they deem clear and credible. Consumers struggle with transparency and trust.

Transparency means giving consumers easy access to the right information at the right time. One in five consumers stated in our core studies that their main barrier to making a sustainable purchase is their lack of knowledge about which products are sustainable. In the absence of such knowledge, consumers tend to rely on proxies to evaluate whether a product or service is sustainable. The most frequently used proxy for a product within consumer goods, automotive sales, and home construction is lifespan or durability, though some consumers look at whether the product is recyclable, reusable, and/or biodegradable or has no excessive packaging. Minimal food waste is another common proxy, as are any details on carbon emissions or other forms of waste.

One company that has built a strong reputation around most of those proxies—durable, recyclable, reusable—is the LEGO Group. Their minimum bar is "durable and long-lasting products that will last at least a lifetime of a child's play needs and usually far beyond that," according to Tim Brooks, the LEGO Group's vice president and global head of sustainability. Brooks added an important nuance that accentuates how durable, recyclable, and reusable LEGO® bricks are when he cited the importance of backward compatibility. "Everything you buy off the shelf today fits together with anything we have made since 1958," Brooks explained, pointing out that he has yet to find another example of such enduring backward compatibility, whether in the digital world or the physical world.[6]

Recyclability may eventually play a role in the production of new bricks and LEGO materials, but the use of nonvirgin plastic presents a challenge, which the LEGO Group's website describes by stressing the criteria that the use of recycled or renewable materials need to meet before being used in manufacturing. "Our ambition," stated Brooks, "is to make LEGO bricks from more sustainable sources without compromising on quality or safety. This is a bold ambition as we need to develop entirely new materials that are safe and strong enough to be passed down through generations. A LEGO brick of the future needs to fit seamlessly with a brick made over 60 years ago."

These efforts from the LEGO Group manifest themselves in the strength of its brand, which helps it overcome consumers' general tendency to mistrust the information they find. This mistrust was a common theme across all archetypes we studied, from nonbelievers to champions. Three in four consumers sometimes or always research a brand because of the risks of greenwashing, and 16 percent of respondents cited lack of trust as their primary barrier to making more sustainable purchases. "You can't trust companies to do whatever they say," said one champion during our focus groups. "You have to investigate it and get third-party verification that they're actually doing what they're saying they're doing."

The level of mistrust increases with a consumer's willingness to pay for sustainable alternatives. In other words, the archetypes that have higher commitments to sustainability and do more research are becoming more mistrustful, not less. This may seem counterintuitive, but it reflects two factors. First, archetypes such as the champions, the image driven, and the thoughtfuls are often conducting research to understand whether a good or service is worth paying for. Second, the greater volume of research they conduct exposes them to a larger number of dubious, confusing, or false claims that make such judgments even harder. The expectations and the research frequency of archetypes such as the skeptics and selectives, in contrast, are much lower. The French retailer Fnac Darty addresses this issue by calculating sustainability scores for different brands and suppliers based on its own data from repairs, maintenance, and installation and displays these scores on its website to help consumers made better selections. We take a closer look at Fnac Darty in chapter 13.

Purchasing Decision

After consumers have defined their trade-offs across potential alternatives, they now decide whether to make a purchase and, if so, which alternative to choose. Tanya, the champion we interviewed, said she will forgo making a purchase if a sustainable option is not available.

For the other archetypes, the mix of sustainability, price, quality, brand, and other factors determine the outcome. Charlotte (cost conscious) and Lucas (selective) said their engagement with sustainability is passive, meaning it is merely a "nice to have" feature broadly related to food, health, or well-being. Sustainability will rarely be a deal breaker for them, but it may be the ultimate factor in decisions that Jennifer (image driven) and Ben (thoughtful) make.

This is where commercial creativity, a core approach we explore in part IV, comes into play. If we keep sustainability's contribution to product value constant at a medium or high level, companies can use different price structures or pricing approaches to make a product more affordable or accessible to a larger number of consumers. Better communication—in the spirit of what our interviews and focus-group participants desire—can enhance brand reputation and over time confer ownership of a sustainable positioning. Improved quality has many dimensions, from better performance to higher efficiency and greater durability.

The lingering impression of many sustainable products, however, is that they are more expensive and deliver less perceived performance than the nonsustainable products they replace. Even when consumers are willing to pay a premium for a sustainable feature, they don't want to end up paying for risk and lower quality as a trade-off. They no longer want "what's good for the planet" and "what's good for me" to demand a trade-off.

User Experience

One of the key insights from our research into consumers is the importance and untapped power of the user experience as a multifaceted source of value for sustainable solutions. We expect the user experience to evolve as a purchase criterion, in the same way that sustainability will evolve, as consumers begin to evaluate a user experience not on its mere presence but on its extent, its intensity, its quality, its lasting impression, and many other factors.

The user experience is the first phase of consumer expansion in our purchasing journey in figure 10.1. It is the opportunity for a company to begin a continuous and trusted relationship with the consumer and enable a strong degree of loyalty and advocacy. It is powerful because it can strongly and directly influence every other part of the purchasing journey. A positive user experience heightens awareness—even about sustainability in general—and keeps a brand in a consumer's consideration set. It redefines a consumer's benchmarks for evaluating alternatives and, in the best case, can alter price–value perceptions to such an extent that the consumer may be willing to pay a premium for their next experience and buy that brand more frequently. Finally, it makes sense that consumers who have repeated positive user experiences will remain loyal and be more willing to serve as brand advocates.

Two aspects of the user experience matter for sustainable solutions. The first is meeting or exceeding expectations through measurable or perceptible performance differences. In theory, every business strives to achieve that goal, but the calculus is currently different with sustainable solutions because they often come with a quality penalty. The parameters for performance difference could range from lower monthly operating expenses and less visible waste in the house to improved health and a higher sense of self-worth for having made the purchase. The latter parameters, however, may be difficult to quantify.

The second aspect is the ongoing reputation of the brand and company. Ongoing communication is essential to help consumers keep their user experience in context, recall it favorably, and enhance it. Other touchpoints such as after-sales service provide opportunities to refresh the positive experience. In contrast, negative news that fosters an impression of greenwashing will reduce the chances that a consumer will make a subsequent purchase, remain loyal, or act as an advocate. But the consumer may continue to use the product in question for the rest of its useful life. One champion justified that action by saying, "I would probably either want to give it away to someone or just keep using it because I'm just making the problem worse by putting it in the garbage, you know?" Champions will tend toward using the product as long as it causes no personal harm.

If the news about the brand or company goes beyond its having made dubious claims, however, consumers may indeed decide to stop using a product. That could happen, say, if the company used child labor or made another egregious violation in the process of making or selling the product. Government agencies punish companies that make unsubstantiated or misleading product claims, but the damage from exposed greenwashing—at least in the court of public opinion— seems to be harsher than the damage from having a "nongreen" claim exposed as false.

Loyalty

Our research shows that consumers are generally more loyal to a sustainable brand than to a nonsustainable brand.[7] One reason is the extensive research consumers conduct to overcome the trust barrier. This greater trust turns sustainability from a competitive advantage that helps a company defend or grow its customer base into one that makes that customer base more valuable. Retaining loyal customers through sustainability commitments will increase share of wallet and customer lifetime value.

One reason for this higher loyalty is the extended evaluation phase, when consumers spend time searching for credible information about the sustainable aspects of a product or brand. They are reluctant to repeat that process again, assuming they have had a positive user experience and no new information has emerged to make them doubt their previous research. When credible information about sustainability is scarce, consumers are more likely to stick with what they already know and trust. "I got a life to live," said one champion. "It's a lot of work to find something that you trust, and once I put in all that work, as long as I don't hear anything different, I'm going to keep going to them." Another Champion echoed that comment: "If I've done the research and I've got the product and I really like the product, I'm going to stick with it and go again."

Sustainability is also more than a purchase criterion. For some consumers, it is part of their identity or self-image, sometimes to the extent that it becomes a lifestyle, which creates an opportunity for companies to integrate a sense of community into their brand image. Around half of consumers say that "feeling good about my purchase" is a motivator to buying sustainable products. Combined with aspects such as social recognition and a desire to act as a role model, this motivator enhances the opportunity for building a community around the brand.

Advocacy

The focus groups and interviews indicated that loyal customers will naturally recommend a brand they like to people in their network. Focusing on advocacy in addition to loyalty can increase the size of the customer base and the share of wallet when people place their trust in a fellow consumer who has already put in the effort to find, vet, and test a solution.

The extent of advocacy will vary by archetype, but consumers seek out and rely on the recommendations and actions of friends, family, and neighbors as well on the recommendations of social media contacts and influencers. This personal network will be important in the early stages of the sustainability megatrend as companies expand their reach, combat mistrust, and educate consumers outside of traditional marketing channels. This process relates strongly to the "from silent to vocal" trend we described in part I.

Consumers see their personal networks as a two-way street. Recall that Lisa (planet saver) said that she will "leave the digital breadcrumbs for the person for whom price is not an object. So if I can't purchase something, I try to promote the product and/or company in ways that hopefully other people can purchase from them." Ben (thoughtful) expressed a desire to serve as a "trusted adviser" and help others learn more about sustainable products and brands.

Taken together, the insights we provided in this part lead us back to the existential challenge we posed in part I: Will you be bold enough to listen to what consumers are saying about sustainability and develop the products to meet their needs? Or will you concede the initiative to companies that will follow a new paradigm of innovation and lock you out of the most lucrative opportunities?

Each company needs to decide what role it wants to play. We believe that the most successful ones will make quick and bold moves to design and market sustainable solutions that meet the demands of consumers in the archetype groups they choose to target. Part IV offers our guidance and recommendations on how to make those bold moves.

IV   The Growth Imperative: How Companies Can Build Successful Strategies around Sustainability

11 The New Innovation Paradigm

As you drive up Interstate 65 toward the border between Kentucky and Indiana, you will notice what seems to be an endless construction site for a new building complex. The scale seems to indicate that the new buildings will form a massive data center or perhaps an e-commerce distribution warehouse, two pillars behind the digitalization megatrend.

The buildings, however, will eventually be pillars of the sustainability megatrend. BlueOval SK, a joint venture between Ford Motor Company and SK Group, South Korea's second-largest industrial conglomerate, or chaebol, has invested $5.8 billion in a complex that will produce advanced batteries for future Ford and Lincoln EVs and create 5,000 new jobs by 2025.[1] Those vehicles include the Ford F-150 Lightning, the electric version of Ford's best-selling F-150 pickup truck.

Ford said in the summer of 2023 that it aimed to produce EVs at an annualized rate of 600,000 vehicles at some point in 2024, after previously saying it could hit the goal in 2023. Ford's CFO John Lawler said, "This is not going to be a straight line. There's going to be some bumpiness as we move along." He added that Ford's challenge in selling EVs was high prices, not consumer interest. In October 2023, he noted that Ford is "trying to find the balance between price, margin and EV demand" and added that "affordability is an issue" for consumers.[2]

Working in Ford's favor is that the F-150 Lightning is more than merely the same pickup truck with an electric drive chain instead of a petroleum-powered one. As a review in the *Wall Street Journal* indicated, the new vehicle may in some ways be superior to its conventionally powered predecessor because of its greater available space and its ability to generate onsite power for tools and other equipment. "May I say, *finally*. An EV that isn't a soft-handed, overpriced toy for white-collar commuters," the review stated. "Something I can use. Actually, the Pro SR looks like a pickup-based business owner's best friend, the tradesman truck to launch a thousand sole proprietorships, thanks to its beautiful circuitry."[3]

Ford's investment in battery development and manufacturing is only one of its big bets to accomplish its sales targets for EVs. In June 2023, the company opened its Cologne Electric Vehicle Center, a "hi-tech production facility in Germany that will build Ford's new generation of electric passenger vehicles for millions of European customers." The transformation of its 93-year-old plant near Cologne is part of an investment of $2 billion in Europe and will be Ford's first carbon-neutral assembly plant in the world.[4]

But more bumpiness in Ford's path may come from Tesla, Chinese manufacturers, and other rival OEMs. Toyota, for example, announced it may be near a breakthrough in solid-state battery technology, which could allow for much faster charging times and longer ranges. The *Financial Times* quoted Peter Bruce, cofounder and chief scientist at the Faraday Institution, as saying that if "Toyota or anyone else succeeds in fabricating solid-state batteries that are cost competitive and deliver the lifetime that is needed, it will be disruptive."[5]

Throughout part IV, we intend to show companies how to look beyond easy fixes and incremental outcomes and instead pursue their own big bets. These are high-reward moves whose risks decrease when companies build them on the ultimate foundation of exponential growth: the world's consumers. One challenge for business leaders is to lower the risk and increase the reward. In other words, they need to make the case for investment more compelling. The necessary response to the demand revolution is large-scale tangible solutions, not more words, empty commitments, and small-scale moves that lead to the failure modes we described in part I. Companies that succeed with these bold moves will help improve the lives of billions of people by unlocking lucrative commercial opportunities.

The question then remains: How should companies direct their innovative and creative energies to capitalize on the demand revolution?

Companies need to follow a new innovation paradigm that will allow rapid responses to pent-up demand. Processes built around traditional adoption patterns—ones that funnel promising new ideas through old processes governed by old strategies with old sets of expectations—are neither fast enough nor ambitious enough.

The three cornerstones of the new innovation paradigm, which we elaborate in the next three sections, are deep consumer focus, rapid product innovation, and innovation of business models and ecosystems. The paradigm demands a balance of commercial creativity and creative destruction. This balance will look much different for incumbents than for sustainability natives, however, because the latter do not have the burden of winding down or retooling assets designed to produce goods that are less sustainable or nonsustainable.

Deep Consumer Focus

As we mentioned in part I, you have probably heard the recommendation "put the customer at the core of your business" a thousand times. It comes up in the first few minutes of any introductory marketing course and is a core recommendation made by most management consultants. But the philosophy of putting customers—or consumers in the case of sustainability—at the core of a company's thinking is the business world's own version of a gap between intention and action. Too few companies do that obsessively day to day, regardless of their plans, their statements, or their good intentions.

The Stanford University professors Jeffrey Pfeffer and Robert Sutton call this break the "knowing–doing" gap. In their book *The Knowing–Doing Gap: How Smart Companies Turn Knowledge into Action*, they write about how David Kelley, cofounder of the design firm IDEO, was surprised "to find that, in firm after firm he visited, executives acted as if merely hearing and talking about methods for doing innovative work eliminated the need to actually use these methods. Kelley's reaction to seeing so much talk and so little action was to give a speech to executives in which he asserted that an obvious, but often ignored, 'secret' to becoming an innovative company is realizing that 'talking about multidisciplinary teams is not enough.'"[6]

In their book *Monetizing Innovation: How Smart Companies Design the Product around the Price*, Madhavan Ramanujam and Georg Tacke reveal the harmful consequences of such knowing–doing gaps. They found that 72 percent of innovations either fail to meet their financial targets or fail entirely. Many companies have come to accept that high failure rate—and the sacrifice of billions of dollars—as simply the cost of doing business. *Monetizing Innovation* argues that this outcome is tragic, wasteful, and wrong. One root cause of it is a lack of customer focus, especially with respect to affordability: "New products fail for many reasons. But the root of all innovation evil . . . is the failure to put the customer's willingness to pay for a new product at the very core of product design. Most companies postpone marketing and pricing decisions to the very end, when they've already developed their new products. They embark on the long and costly journey of product development hoping they'll make money on their innovations, but not at all knowing if they will."[7]

The perception gap that we showed in figure 2.1 would also be much narrower if companies designed innovations with consumers in mind at the core instead of just intending to put them there. Companies should listen to what consumers think about sustainability—as we documented thoroughly in part III—instead of buying into the green mirage and shaming consumers for the alleged disconnect between their desire for sustainability and their willingness to pay a premium for it.

Product Innovation That Reflects a Sustainability Strategy

One of the many difficulties in adopting a new innovation paradigm is an entrenched bias toward the supply side at the expense of the demand side.

The long-term success of any business hinges on its ability to develop and launch superior products at scale. In theory, superior products—ones with higher perceived value for consumers—ought to win the largest market share and the largest share of a market's profit pool. That aspiration seems obvious, but the challenge lies in determining what superior means—that is, in choosing the right measurement criteria.

One of the failure modes we described in part I is "If it's green, it's good enough." A company may be superior in terms of having a sustainable feature or "being green," but its success chances are much lower—certainly at scale—if consumers perceive the product to be otherwise inferior as they weigh other value drivers such as price, quality, and brand. That perception may be a result of product performance. In other cases, a company has a superior product, but it is held back by factors related to the demand side: ineffective communication, a suboptimal positioning, a channel strategy that limits convenient access, or a pricing strategy that creates an unattractive price–value relationship.

Companies can choose one of three strategies for sustainable product innovation, depending on their target archetypes and the trade-offs that consumers in those archetypes are willing to make. Independent of which strategy they choose, companies should achieve and communicate how their offerings reduce waste or enhance efficiency, a theme that all eight archetypes expressed in common, even the nonbelievers. Companies should follow the paths of least resistance for their target archetypes, as we described in part I. The three strategies for sustainable product innovation are:

- **Sustainable and superior:** The underlying thinking is "sustainable and . . ."; by integrating environmental sustainability into the company's product-innovation roadmap, the company creates an offering that is superior to alternatives, whether they are sustainable or not. Such an offering creates opportunities to price flexibly for scale or to extract more of the willingness to pay in certain target archetypes, such as the image driven and the champions, or to attract archetypes that place relatively high emphasis on quality, such as the cost conscious and the selectives.

- **Sustainable at parity:** Based on what we heard in our focus groups, the sustainability of products breaks ties in the minds of consumers. The company creates sustainable products that consumers are likely to choose over the traditional products, if everything else is at parity in terms of other value drivers such as price, quality, and design. The company may not be able to extract added value from any archetype, even with commercial creativity, which makes volume and rapid scale more important as ways to keep the cost base competitive. These products appeal to consumers who have a stronger affinity to sustainability, primarily the champions and the thoughtfuls, but can also attract more price-sensitive archetypes because price parity implies affordability.

- **Sustainable with trade-offs:** Companies can be superior in some attributes, such as sustainability, but inferior in other attributes, such as design. Engineering these trade-offs may keep production costs low enough to enable a company to charge a competitive price. However, such products will appeal only to those consumers willing to accept sacrifices or tough trade-offs, such as the planet savers.

The new paradigm will spawn a wave of innovation—either from incumbents or from new companies—beyond the narrow terms of new-product development. We anticipate groundbreaking business model innovations and commercial creativity in how companies take their solutions to market. We also anticipate fundamental shifts in how companies organize themselves within larger ecosystems instead of along traditional value-chain partnerships.

Laundry sheets, a new entrant to the detergent category, currently fall into the second and third categories but have the potential to be sustainable and superior in the long term. The emergence of laundry sheets as a viable alternative to liquid detergent eliminates the need for a company to ship plastic bottles and large amounts of water across large distances. As the US magazine *Consumer Reports* stated, the use of sheets across the board would get rid of "the plastic detergent-bottle kettlebells we struggle to lift off shelves."[8] A large-scale switch to sheets would also eliminate large amounts of physical waste. The US Environmental Protection Agency has estimated the amount of municipal waste from plastic containers and packaging at more than 14.5 million tons per year.[9] The benefits of laundry sheets extend beyond physical waste. The prices offered by some suppliers make them competitive with conventional detergents. Sheets are also easy to use and easy to store. Unilever has entered the market for laundry sheets and calls them an "ultra-convenient, sustainable format."[10]

The sheets' performance, however, currently leaves them short of the "sustainable and superior" level. *Good Housekeeping* tested 24 sheets from 20 brands and came to a more positive conclusion in its rankings but still cited pros and cons for all brands tested.[11] *Consumer Reports* rigorously tested several laundry sheets, compared them with conventional products, and found them to perform worse on harder-to-clean stains. Its conclusion was that "if you're organizing your home around a sustainable lifestyle—and your laundry isn't heavily soiled—laundry sheets may be a viable option. For instance, you could use the strips for routine loads, and save the traditional liquid or pod detergent for deeper cleaning—using a minimal amount per load and increasing the dose only for dirtier items."[12]

Innovating and Expanding Business Models and Ecosystems

This leads to the third cornerstone of the new innovation paradigm, which is the innovation, renovation, or expansion of business models and ecosystems. Business models have expiration dates, and those dates will arrive sooner when consumers have pent-up demand that companies cannot tap with traditional approaches. Many profitable business models also still depend on waste, including the encouragement of excess consumption, often supported by production processes that may be efficient but not necessarily environmentally or socially favorable.

For many companies, bringing a sustainable product or service alternative to market means reorganizing and redesigning entire value chains. For some, this process will be an evolution, but for others, such as fast-fashion and fossil-fuel companies, it will be a revolution. Some companies will need to divest, reposition, or shut down some operations to free up necessary resources to reinvest in their sustainable transformation.

Companies may also not be able to serve consumers on their own. They need to keep in mind that the world's most challenging problems, many related to sustainability, are too big for a single company or even a single industry to solve lucratively on its own. "No government or organization can solve climate change alone," the World Economic Forum wrote in March 2023. "The scale and urgency of the emergency requires the pooling of resources, knowledge, people power and strategies. In this way, businesses can collectively lead the way towards a carbon-neutral future. Put simply, a carbon-neutral world requires 'all hands on deck'" so that companies can accelerate progress and share the burden of innovation.[13] The risk in such statements, however, is that when no single organization can solve a problem alone, no one makes the first move to set a standard. Tesla defied that risk by rolling out its own standard for EV battery charging. Ford announced that it will adopt Tesla's North American Charging Standard starting in 2024, which gives Ford EV owners access to Tesla's network of charging stations.[14]

Tesla has embraced the new innovation paradigm from the very start as a new entrant into the automotive industry. It's one thing to bring a zero-emission EV to market, but quite another to introduce a better vehicle powered by electricity at an affordable price and supported by its own ecosystem in terms of sales, service, and charging stations. A survey of US consumers by *Consumer Reports* stressed the importance of such an ecosystem as a purchase criterion for EVs. Some 36 percent of respondents said they would "definitely" or "seriously" consider choosing an EV the next time they buy a car, but the biggest purchase barrier—cited by 61 percent of the respondents—was the logistics of charging the vehicles.[15] The stronger the supporting ecosystem becomes, the lower the adoption barriers are for customers.

In the broader market for EVs, however, the perception gap we showed in figure 2.1 persists, as a survey conducted by Cox Automotive in 2023 revealed. "Less than a third of the 152 dealers surveyed by Cox say they think EVs are the future and will largely replace gasoline vehicles over time," according to a report in *Automotive News*. The report added that around half of those dealers feel that EVs need time to prove themselves.[16]

Consumers see the situation much differently. Cox also surveyed 1,024 consumers and found that 53 percent of them "feel that EVs are the future" compared to just 31 percent of dealers. Cox also reports that 51 percent of consumers will consider an EV purchase in the next 12 months—compared to 38 percent in Cox's survey a year earlier—because they see many advantages, including fuel savings, environmental impact, performance, maintenance efficiency, and lower cost of ownership. Cox cites education as the difference maker: "Education for both consumers and dealers remains a critical factor in driving widespread confidence and adoption of electric vehicles."[17]

How much a company can do on its own—and how it can work well with other organizations—depends on an honest assessment of its own innovative capacity, its ability to bring solutions to market quickly, and its ability to attract capital and consumers with its powerful messages. Sectors are much more intertwined than before, and processes are dynamic rather than linear. As the example of Tesla, Ford, and the North American Charging Standard shows, most companies will need to enter alliances or join ecosystems instead of relying primarily on their own resources.

To bring successful solutions to market, it may even be necessary for companies to look beyond their own value chain and enter into alliances with players from their own industry and even from other industries. That could turn competitors into partners, for example, in establishing uniform standards for a sustainable or reusable bottle, such as the ones pioneered by the Loop platform.[18] In these extended ecosystems, each company needs to decide whether it will be the spider, a strand in the web, or part of the frame that supports the web. No matter their position, companies in an ecosystem rely on collaboration and coordination among the various stakeholders.

Maersk, for example, now has on order 25 vessels with engines powered by green methanol, which has relatively low greenhouse-gas emissions compared to fossil fuels. But supporting that conversion at scale requires extensive infrastructure. "To manufacture methanol, transport methanol, distribute methanol, [and] have it available in most of the ports . . . I need competitors to join me on the methanol journey and think that this is the way to go in order to decarbonize," said Vincent Clerc, the CEO of Maersk. "If we don't get followership, it doesn't matter that our solution is better," he added. "It just won't work. And so we have had to really engage with the ecosystem to get followership today."[19]

Commercial Creativity Meets Creative Destruction

Traditional business models and business strategies are not well designed for companies to seize the exponential growth opportunities for sustainable solutions in their markets. This makes any industry an ideal candidate for the forces of commercial creativity and creative destruction, which will inspire companies to make bold moves with urgency.

Commercial Creativity

Commercial creativity covers the ability to innovate business models quickly and effectively to bring successful sustainable solutions to market. Broadly speaking, it encompasses a company's willingness and ability to reengineer every cylinder of its revenue engine in response to consumer demand.[20] The creativity comes in as companies seek to break away from traditional approaches as they break down the consumer affordability, accessibility, knowledge, and trust barriers.

To develop sustainable products, companies need to collaborate with their customers to understand their demands. But to market those products, companies need to understand that consumers are generally suspicious of sustainability claims and will invest their own time and effort to validate them. Consumers need to know how and why the offering will make both them and others better off. In an environment of suspicion, companies need to invest not only in making their products or services superior and sustainable but also in convincing consumers that their claims are genuine. They need to communicate and price creatively to make their offerings attractive and reduce those cost burdens over time.

Such suspicions—and the resulting challenges—extend beyond day-to-day consumer activities and can even create marketing challenges in fields such as asset management. "You can argue actual margins might be reduced for the asset-management and investment industry because clear reporting standards, marketing materials, and the additional information which need to be provided to demonstrate that these portfolios and investment products are indeed sustainable will inevitably add cost," said Jan-Marc Fergg, the global head of ESG & Managed Solutions at HSBC.[21] Consumers are also active in new channels for information (e.g., social media) and new sales channels (e.g., online and secondhand) that may be more reliable and convenient for them than conventional channels.

When a company fills the leadership vacuum in its industry or category, it has an opportunity to become a perceived sustainability leader in the same way that industries and categories have price, quality, and brand leaders as well as leaders on specific features such as safety. The digitalization megatrend unleashed a wave of commercial creativity with new pricing models, new channels, and new forms of communication, many of them pioneered by digital natives. In the sustainability megatrend, companies will need to do the same, either by discovering new means or borrowing or transferring proven business models from another industry. They will also need to reimagine alliances and ecosystems instead of relying primarily on their own limited resources. In some cases, they will merge several categories together into one product and business model, which is what the smartphone exemplifies. It combines several established industries—telephony, photography, gaming, entertainment, and, to a lesser extent, navigation and timekeeping—into one device, without the need for mobile-device companies to destroy an existing way of doing business.

Creative Destruction

Creative destruction, as defined by Joseph Schumpeter, refers to the "process of industrial mutation that continuously revolutionizes the economic structure from within, incessantly destroying the old one, incessantly creating a new one."[22] Just as digitalization unleashed waves of commercial creativity, it also brought about waves of creative destruction. The fates of Kodak, Blockbuster, the printed newspaper, and the compact disc (CD) serve as classic cautionary tales about how business models can disappear quickly, taking fortunes with them, unless business leaders respond with commercial creativity.

Both *commercial creativity* and *creative destruction* share the word *create*, which marks an intimate link between the two ideas, and also with the goal of value creation. It also marks the fine line between life or death for companies when old markets dry up as adjacent ones take root. Neither creative destruction nor commercial creativity happens on its own, but a transformation cannot happen without either one. Each occurs solely through the action or inaction of businesses. Companies will struggle to implement new ideas if they can't wind down old ideas at the same time, no matter how successful those old ideas were in their heyday or how bold the new ideas are.

A company's optimal balance of commercial creativity and creative destruction will depend on the extent of its own current perception gap, the pent-up demand in its market, and its opportunities for first-mover advantages to achieve exponential growth with speed and scale. Figure 11.1 shows this balance.

Because the sustainability megatrend is still emerging, and only few companies have managed to close their perception gap, we illustrate the different combinations in figure 11.1 with insights from the digitalization megatrend and draw some connections to sustainability.

Automotive OEMs may be in the upper-right corner of the matrix. Much of their ecosystem—from sales to service—depends on the modern automobile as it exists today. Commercial creativity should lead them to investigate new revenue streams, focus on different channels, build new supporting infrastructure, and find the right partners within

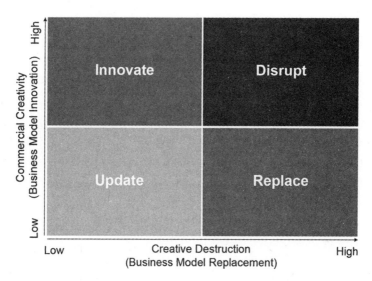

Figure 11.1
Balancing commercial creativity and creative destruction.

a redefined extended ecosystem. Creative destruction in the automotive industry, meanwhile, will affect the displacement not only of internal combustion engines (ICEs) by electric power trains but also of the broader ecosystem that ICEs support. A report in *Automotive News* in May 2023, citing S&P Global Mobility, stated that ICE "suppliers need to relearn how to swim—or risk sinking—as the EV transition begins." The question of balance comes up as automotive OEMs look for ways to repurpose the ICEs and extend their useful life. According to another report in *Automotive News*, one way is to develop e-fuels, which "combines carbon dioxide taken from the atmosphere—or captured at the source, such as at a refinery—and hydrogen obtained from water through electrolysis."[23]

Online music-streaming services also exemplify a high degree of commercial creativity and creative destruction. The change from buying CDs and cassette tapes in music stores to instant access to music online is a remarkable shift in how people listen to music. Commercial creativity came through in the change to subscription-based revenue models, personalized recommendations through data analytics, and collaboration with artists and brands for advertisements catered to different audiences. These changes broke down barriers to affordability and access and created new opportunities for artists and fans to interact. At the same time, extensive creative destruction also occurred. Traditional distribution channels disappeared as sales of the once-dominant CD format plummeted. Although once-extinct formats such as vinyl have staged a comeback, streaming now represents around two-thirds of the recorded music industry's global revenue of around $26 billion, after accounting for essentially no revenue at all two decades ago.[24]

12   Are You Dead Yet?

A business leader's toughest sustainability challenge right now is not how fast the climate is changing but how fast market demand is changing and how fast the business needs to change as a result.

To ignite exponential growth from sustainability—growth that is long overdue—companies need to sell to a critical mass of consumers. But before they can accomplish that, they need to make an external and internal assessment of their readiness and urgency. This statement explains the blunt and provocative title for this chapter. The answer to the question is, we hope, "No, we're not dead yet," but its intent is to start an open, honest, and necessary discussion about the creative destruction that will overtake nearly every industry.

Consultants often face the accusation that they scare clients into action by stressing the risks of a current strategy and thus artificially creating urgency. But as sustainability becomes a transformative megatrend, there will be no need to create artificial urgency. One irrefutable lesson from previous transformative megatrends is that they won't be victimless. Companies and product categories die if they do not make the transition to an emerging transformative megatrend. Countless companies, business units, research activities, and sales channels have disappeared since digitalization took hold.

But whether a company becomes a victim is usually a choice, not an inevitability, as long as the company continues to listen to consumers and provide the experiences they want. When existing business models have expiration dates, a company's future success depends on whether business leaders are bold enough to shift away from current models and build a more profitable future before it is too late. They need to figure out how much time they have left to initiate the controlled inside-out destruction of old ways of doing business. Technologies can slide quickly into irrelevance unless the company can make a transition to a new way of doing business. Sales of fax machines, for example, declined by 94 percent between 1997 and 2010 in dollar terms.[1] Companies also have different sensitivities to these shifts. Some can apply commercial creativity quickly and survive a 10–30 percent loss of revenue or volume, but a loss of that magnitude may prove fatal for other companies.

At workshops in the early 2000s, some of our colleagues would introduce the topic of technological convergence and expiring business models by asking participants which experience they would prefer most: playing games on their camera, taking pictures with their phone, or making phone calls from their gaming device? The combinations would vary from workshop to workshop, but they always inspired fascinating discussions. In hindsight, they also indicated a white space that one company (Apple) filled less than a decade later with a single device that does all three.

Blockbuster and Kodak are the poster children for what happens when companies do not adapt to fundamental shifts in consumer demand and preferences. Although it is easy to assume their competitors—Netflix, Sony, Apple, Fujifilm—took each of them out with one massive blind-side punch, the underlying stories of Blockbuster and Kodak reveal a more nuanced tension between commercial creativity and creative destruction.

Blockbuster had proven that people wanted private access to movies. By the late 1990s, Blockbuster had more than 9,000 stores and 65 million registered customers.[2] Then Netflix launched a service that was less expensive, offered more liberal return policies, and had more titles to choose from. In the earliest iteration of Netflix, consumers made the trade-off between going to the store to select a movie or waiting until the DVD arrived in the mail. By the time Netflix had accumulated 65 million subscribers of its own in 2015, Blockbuster was long gone, having filed for bankruptcy in 2010.[3]

How did Blockbuster try to prevent this outcome? In a *Harvard Business Review* article published in April 2011, the former Blockbuster CEO John Antioco gave his firsthand account of his battles with the activist investor Carl Icahn for control of the company. Within his lengthy and detailed account of the proxy fight with Icahn, Antioco nicely frames up the tensions that Blockbuster faced as it adjusted to the entry of Netflix and the industry's format shift from VHS cassettes to DVDs. One move was to get movie studios to agree to a revenue-sharing model instead of charging Blockbuster a high one-time price to purchase the VHS cassettes it rented. That move allowed Blockbuster to expand its inventory and prevent stock outs. "Comp store sales and market share grew strongly," Antioco wrote.[4]

In August 2004, Blockbuster entered the online business and changed its pricing model by eliminating late fees, which were a big source of profits but which customers "hated." The company also wanted to acquire Hollywood Video in 2004 with the goal to "orchestrate an orderly downsizing of its store-based business and take on its customers as our own while we also focused on developing alternative movie-delivery methods." The activist investor questioned the strategy of "growing an online business and finding new ways to satisfy customers, like getting rid of late fees." When Antioco left the company in 2007 after the proxy fight, Blockbuster reversed course. In his words, "Blockbuster Online was growing incredibly fast and we had successfully slowed Netflix's momentum, [but CEO James] Keyes made it very public that management planned to drastically change the strategy. The company announced a big price increase for online customers, cut way back on marketing, and decided to intensify the focus on the store-based business." When Antioco published his article in 2011, he felt that "if our online strategy had not been essentially abandoned, Blockbuster Online would have 10 million subscribers today, and we'd be rivaling Netflix for the leadership position in the internet downloading business."[5]

Kodak's efforts to compete—first against digital-camera rivals and then against the smartphone—likewise show a concerted mix of commercial creativity and creative destruction. But the company's leaders ultimately faced a challenge with no simple answer and few if any precedents: How do you kill a company's beloved golden goose before it dies a natural death anyway?

For the majority of the twentieth century, Eastman Kodak dominated the photography market, at one point selling 90 percent of the film consumed in the United States. The company was still growing in 2005, when its revenue increased by 6 percent to $14.27 billion.[6] However, the rise of digital photography and ultimately the rise of the smartphone took its toll on Kodak, and the company filed for bankruptcy in 2012.[7] Robert Burley, a professor of photography at Ryerson University in Toronto, described Kodak's fate in 2012: "Kodak has been obliterated by the creative destruction of a digital age. Like many of its competitors, it appears unable to make the transition into the 21st century. Five years ago, it was unthinkable that this American business legend would find itself in a bankruptcy position. Kodak was caught in a perfect storm of not only technological, but also social and economic change."[8]

Kodak appears to be a perfect example of a victim of the digitalization megatrend. But in an article in the *MIT Sloan Management Review* in May 2016, Willy Shih, who once led Kodak's stand-alone digital division, presents a more nuanced view of what happened. He calls the stories about Kodak missing the technology shift from analog to digital "wrong" and the criticisms of Kodak's management for dismissing digital opportunities and protecting the film business "overblown." One of Kodak's responses to enter the digital-camera market was to create its own digital native, a camera unit that was not "constrained by any legacy assets or practices." That unit's products held a leading market share position in 2005. It proved that Kodak could replace the film camera with a digital one and hold its own, at least until smartphones with built-in cameras fully democratized consumer photography. But Kodak felt it couldn't replace film, and film was the lifeblood of what

Shih called a "unique and powerful" ecosystem built around how consumers used the product. The majority of Kodak's profits came from manufacturing and selling film, and its retail partners made large profits from photo finishing.[9]

One of the trends we described in chapter 2—from atomistic to holistic value—unraveled that ecosystem when film was no longer necessary for consumers. Democratized digital photography turned a multistep process of obtaining a photo into an instant single-step one. It eliminated many consumer trips to retail partners or to stand-alone kiosks to buy film, bring in pictures for development, and pick them up later, all the while filling their shopping baskets with other products. When film sales disappeared, so did the relationships within that ecosystem.

Kodak's Japanese rival Fujifilm faced similar challenges, but it followed a different strategy. It killed its own golden goose—photographic film—by diversifying heavily into cameras and other film applications. As the former Fujifilm chairman and CEO Shigetaka Komori writes in his book *Innovating out of Crisis: How Fujifilm Survived (and Thrived) as Its Core Business Was Vanishing*, the pending plunge in photographic film revenues forced his company's hand: "It was clear to me that this was not the time for makeshift measures. Our only choice was to initiate radical reform, including the downsizing of our photography-related businesses. Had we delayed by just another year or two, we would have been right in the middle of the devastating financial downturn in the fall of 2008 and the company might not have been able to survive." He adds that "if we had not done it, another company eventually would. There was basically no choice." Komori credited Kodak for its attempts to diversify into sectors such as health care, but he noted that "there was a big difference in the depth and breadth of our execution."[10] By the time Komori resigned in 2021, Fujifilm had transformed itself into a company earning more than half of its revenues from health care and materials.

Kodak generated $1.2 billion in revenues in 2022, with traditional and digital printing still contributing 78 percent of its revenue.[11] For its 2022 fiscal year, Fujifilm was more than 15 times larger than Kodak in terms of revenue. It posted roughly $20 billion in revenues, with health care accounting for around one-third of the total and imaging less than 15 percent of the total.[12]

What else could Kodak have done? That question is a subhead in Shih's article, and he wrote that Kodak could have used strengths that underpinned its film business, such as expertise in complex organic chemistry and high-speed coating. In other words, the company could have used its strengths to enter new markets. He acknowledged that Fuji successfully followed that path, but for Kodak it "would have meant walking away from a great consumer franchise. That's not the logic that managers learn at business schools, and it would have been a hard pill for Kodak leaders to swallow."[13]

The contrast between Fujifilm and Kodak not only shows the combined power of commercial creativity and creative destruction but also shows that bold moves can work, that core legacy capabilities can be a boon rather than a burden, and that rapid growth in new markets is not the exclusive domain of "natives" who do not need to overcome the biases and inertia of an existing organization.

Who Will Be the Victims of the Sustainability Megatrend?

Tesla is taking significant market share from several auto manufacturers, and not all manufacturers, divisions, and brands will survive. Some will survive, but many of them will be diminished. Historically, that is nothing new. Automakers in the United States have a history of bankruptcies, with a large shakeout in the 1950s and 1960s. In recent years, Chrysler, Ford, and General Motors have eliminated once iconic brands such as Plymouth, Mercury, and Oldsmobile.

More broadly speaking, will big oil companies die unless they transition into sustainable energy solutions? What is the likelihood that they otherwise won't be huge companies in the next 10 to 30 years? Moves by Chevron in 2023 indicate that the oil giants have no intent to slow down their fossil-fuel production in the medium term, despite the International Energy Agency's forecast that the world is at "the beginning of the end" of the fossil-fuel era and that demand for oil, natural gas, and coal will peak before 2030.[14] Chevron announced a bid in October 2023 to buy Hess Corp. for $53 billion. Chevron CEO Mike Wirth told the *Financial Times* in an interview prior to that bid that his company is "selling a product that has changed the quality of life on this planet. For the better."[15] The editorial board of the *Wall Street Journal* echoed Wirth's comments when it said that the "real threat to a more prosperous future, as Chevron well knows, is a world with too little oil and gas, not too much."[16]

If companies move too slowly, newcomers will seize the opportunities. It seems inevitable that a new wave of "megatrend natives"—companies that arise as a direct consequence of a megatrend—will emerge around sustainability and transform industries, as Tesla is doing. Neither Amazon nor Facebook nor Google existed before digitalization, but a generation later each reached a market capitalization of more than $1 trillion. Tesla's market capitalization exceeded $1 trillion for the first time on October 25, 2021.[17]

What sustainability natives will follow the kinds of trajectories that these digital natives did? Bill Gates said in October 2021 that he expects investments in climate change alone to create "eight Teslas, 10 Teslas" as well as additional "Microsoft, Google, Amazon-type companies."[18] The Blackrock CEO Larry Fink made a similar kind of forecast at a conference in Riyadh, Saudi Arabia, the same week: "It is my belief that the next 1,000 unicorns—companies that have a market valuation over a billion dollars—won't be a search engine, won't be a media company, they'll be businesses developing green hydrogen, green agriculture, green steel and green cement."[19]

How Companies Determine Their Next Steps

Survival is not success. A company still needs to shift its course to the upper curve in figure 2.1 by eliminating its perception gap and getting ahead of the curve, literally and figuratively. Determining its next steps will require asking itself these three questions:

- **How advanced are our consumers?** Market opportunities will emerge at different speeds, depending on the clarity of consumer needs across archetypes, the intensity of their demands, and their willingness to back up their demands with money and purchase volume when a company offers them the right solutions. Finding the answer to this question will help the company qualitatively and quantitatively assess the pent-up demand in an industry, market, or a category. A company should also look at combinations of the eight archetypes, not just at each archetype in isolation, to find its largest target market.

- **How advanced are our competitors?** Companies need to understand where their industry and competitors are positioned within the demand revolution to understand the competitive urgency to make a bold move. In a few industries, the revolution is in full force right now. In some, it is still intensifying, while in others it remains on the fringes. The answer to this question provides indications of the extent of commercial creativity and creative destruction that certain moves will require. In other words, the answer will help the company position itself in figure 12.1.

- **How ready are we to use the new innovation paradigm?** The answers to the first two questions establish a market's level of maturity in terms of sustainability. On that basis, a company can start to design the solutions that will enable it to achieve scale quickly. It can also define changes to its business model and go-to-market strategies to make sure those solutions reach consumers, provide them with the experience they demand, and build loyalty and advocacy. It can also define the kind of ecosystem that will support the rapid scaling of the solution.

We now look at these three questions in greater detail.

How Advanced Are Our Consumers?

When companies replace consumer frustrations with better consumer experiences, they can tap into the pent-up demand and generate even more demand. Awareness alone can spark or renew a consumer's passion for sustainability.

In chapter 10, we emphasized the importance of consumer experience. Amazon built its success as a digital native around defining a better customer experience, using a process it refers to as "working backwards," which means a team will "start by defining the customer experience, then iteratively work backwards from that point until the team achieves clarity of thought around what to build."[20]

To define these new experiences, a company needs the most comprehensive view of its consumers right now as well as insights into how rapidly they are changing. The company needs to explore and quantify which way its customers are headed in terms of archetype, size, needs, willingness to pay, and the barriers and motivators they face to adoption, which will help the company understand *why* its consumers are heading that way and what paths to adopting sustainable solutions offer the least resistance.

The importance of sustainability as a value driver and a purchase criterion varies by industry, product, and archetype. While our survey showed its importance to be strong and robust in general, specific breakdowns are critical for an individual company to plan the timing and intensity of its response to the demand and thus to determine how boldly and aggressively it can act to win consumers. These perspectives will give the company a clear picture of the extent of pent-up demand and its growth potential. This knowledge should make business leaders and investors confident that they are not pursuing fringe opportunities with a highly uncertain return.

How Advanced Are Our Competitors?

Companies need to review their competitive position under two assumptions. The first is that their most aggressive competitor in both the medium term and the long term may not exist yet. The second is that radical change will come quickly as the demand revolution affects their industry. They need to know who will lead that change, who will prosper from it, and who won't.

Assessing the positions and movements of competitors means determining what their perception gaps look like by drawing inferences from
their product portfolios, how they market their products, how well they
are performing commercially and financially, how they position themselves, and how well that positioning resonates with consumers. With
this assessment, a company can also judge whether its own needs for
creative destruction are manageable relative to its competitors' needs.
It can see what consequences creative destruction may have, such as
restricting access to outside capital or diverting funds that could be
invested instead in sustainable experiences.

We assume that for most markets right now no company owns the
sustainability positioning, which means there is a leadership vacuum.
New products enter the market through the conventional innovation
paradigm, which means they tend to have the same price models in the
same sales channels as the products they are replacing. Thus, they labor
under the constraints and fallacies of the green mirage. In other cases,
such as the market for EVs, there are fewer products and companies in
failure modes. One company has already filled the leadership vacuum,
and companies are applying different pricing strategies, using new sales
channels, and revamping their communications strategies to reach
consumers. Incumbents such as Ford are managing creative destruction
by retooling existing assets.

In each case, a competitor will have a set of opportunities that it can
seize first with the new innovation paradigm: faster consumer-focused
product development, new business models and go-to-market strategies, and a new ecosystem to support consumers, suppliers, and the
company as the solution scales. It will also have a set of opportunities
where it could gain from becoming a fast follower. The hardest part
may be to anticipate the arrival of sustainability natives—or even to
create one if it can identify opportunities ideally suited for a company
with the freedom to exercise a high level of commercial creativity and
little or no need for internal creative destruction. When an incumbent
views an opportunity with this native mentality, it may find other
ways to adapt and respond flexibly as it undertakes bold initiatives.

As the incumbent does that, it also needs to be aware that its move in one industry can affect companies in other industries and potentially unravel an established ecosystem. The choices made by automotive manufacturers and their balance of commercial creativity and creative destruction, for example, will have consequences for the future of service stations.

In the United States, however, the service-station sector is undergoing a transformation as chains of megastores such as BUC-EE's and Wally's spread across the country. BUC-EE's opened a convenience store outside of Knoxville, Tennessee, in 2023 with a world-record 74,000 square feet of space and 120 fuel pumps. For comparison, the soccer pitch at Wembley Stadium in London is 76,590 square feet, and a standard American football field, with end zones, is 57,240 square feet. The new facility breaks BUC-EE's previous world record, held by its store in New Braunfels, Texas, which has 66,335 square feet of space.[21]

Why is a company building so many massive fueling stations for ICE vehicles when the trend seems to be away from such vehicles? The facility in Texas may offer the answer. The BUC-EE's in New Braunfels also has 24 Tesla charging stations.[22] It seems that BUC-EE's plans to be well positioned to serve any driver, regardless of their vehicle. But traditional gas stations closer to a driver's residence may not have the volume that BUC-EE's will have due to its locations along major highways. When consumers charge their EVs at home, their need to stop at a local service station and visit its convenience store diminishes.

How Ready Are We to Use the New Innovation Paradigm?

The assessment of the market maturity—both the value of consumers and the industry urgency—will set the strategic ambition for an accelerated sustainability transition. The third step for companies is to assess their own internal readiness: What will it take for them to seize the emerging market opportunities in their industry and create more value?

A company needs to compare the products and services that customers want—and for which they have pent-up demand—against the current portfolio and the products it has under development. It also needs to assess how well it can overcome the barriers to adoption. Each barrier lends itself to commercial creativity. To improve affordability, a company can take a radical look at how to cut costs, such as simplifying manufacturing processes, or at how to change the nature of the product. It can also change the basis behind its price model or use subscriptions or freemium models to enable consumers to experience the new solutions.

Accessibility corresponds to channel strategy, and it may compel some companies to reconsider common approaches, such as having an omnichannel presence. Rapid scaling and success for sustainable products may come more from being in the right channels, not in the most channels. Knowledge and trust involve communication, which starts with value proposition and brand and filters down to heavier use of alternative channels, such as social media. The supporting ecosystem has a role to play in supporting all these areas. Simplifying a channel structure by removing layers can improve affordability and accessibility simultaneously.

By juxtaposing this internal assessment of readiness with the market maturity, a company can begin to estimate the optimal balance of commercial creativity and creative destruction to achieve its strategic ambition. It will have a clear view on how to close the perception gap, move to the upper curve of exponential growth, and unlock the commercial opportunities associated with the sustainability megatrend.

Consumers need help from companies in many ways to start, advance, or accelerate their own journeys. By estimating their pent-up demand, identifying opportunities to seize a first- or early-mover advantage, and understanding their own readiness, companies can now plan more precisely on how to follow the new innovation paradigm. To guide them, we have developed six strategic plays that they can initiate in isolation or in combination. Our primary goal with these strategic plays, shown in figure 12.1, is to motivate and inspire companies that seek to win the consumers in their market. Each play reflects specific strategic and

Brand Play Achieve a market-leader sustainability positioning in the minds of consumers	**Longevity Play** Develop products that are designed to last to give products second or third lives
Mass Affordability Play Reach scale to offer sustainable solutions at prices aligned with mass affordability thresholds 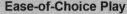	**Ease-of-Choice Play** Make sustainable solutions easy to choose by increasing access to products and information
Engagement Play Incentivize consumers to accelerate their sustainable purchases through closer engagement and experiences	**Antiwaste Play** Innovate production cycles and product offering around an antiwaste principle

Figure 12.1
The six strategic plays companies can make to win over consumers with speed and at scale.

commercial approaches that will enable companies to unlock the rapidly developing commercial opportunity of sustainability.

We explore these strategic plays in depth in the final three chapters, which bring together all the ideas and insights from the preceding chapters. Chapter 13 introduces the longevity play and the brand play, both of which are linked to universal purchasing criteria of brand and quality but also include sustainability as an integral part of the consumer's purchase decision. Chapter 14 introduces the mass affordability and antiwaste plays, in which price also plays a prominent role as a value driver. The antiwaste play also addresses a core consumer frustration shared to some extent by all archetypes. Chapter 15 introduces the ease-of-choice and engagement plays, which home in on how companies can activate their consumers before, during, and after the sale.

Following the Growth Imperative

The companies we highlight in chapters 13–15 range from well-known global leaders to smaller companies with new initiatives showing early signs of success. They are active in sectors from apparel and retail to food and beverage to transportation and entertainment. But they all have two things in common.

First, they are creating value by following the imperatives of the demand revolution that we defined in chapters 1 and 3. They are putting consumers first by listening and by understanding how their needs are both diverse and in constant flux. They are following a different innovation paradigm, one that goes beyond the traditional manufacturing of products and considers the business model and the entire ecosystem. They have implemented new ways to go to market and support those efforts with clear communication.

Second, they are capitalizing on the trends that we showed in figure 4.2, including the shift from volume to value, the shift from a linear to a circular economy, and the shift from excess waste to antiwaste. They know that one or more of these trends offer their target consumers a path of least resistance to leading a more sustainable lifestyle. Sustainability doesn't stop when a consumer purchases a product or service. The more consumers focus on circularity and recyclability, for example, the more they compel companies to replace their linear value chains with circular ones designed for extended reuse and a maximum degree of recycling.

Each of these chapters also begins with an aspirational viewpoint. These "moonshots" are the outputs of imagination at scale, showing how ideas can push boundaries, change economies, and change the daily lives of hundreds of millions—if not billions—of people.

Some large companies or governments are investing heavily in such moonshots. Toyota conceived Woven City, an experimental city near Mount Fuji, as a place to "conduct trials of new ideas for systems and services that expand mobility and unlock human potential."[23] Saudi Arabia has begun construction of the city of Neom under the guidance of "a community of the brightest minds committed to reimagining what a sustainable future will look like in 20 to 30 years, and building it today."[24] Switzerland has an ambitious plan dubbed Cargo Sous Terrain, which its Federal Office of Transport calls "fully-automatic underground freight transport between the major urban centres."[25] The privately funded effort will shift freight from railways and roads to a system of tunnels, with cargo moving on self-driving pods. The Office of Transport claims the project will reduce heavy road traffic by up to 40 percent and emit 80 percent less CO_2 per ton of cargo compared to road transport.[26] Even if the moonshots never fulfill their missions, the by-products of the thought process often yield other practical ways to create value and improve people's lives.

Companies need to make a full commitment to whatever play or combination of plays they select and follow the four imperatives. If a company implements a play without that full commitment—or implements no play at all—it risks backsliding into failure modes and leaving an exponential-growth opportunity on the table for someone else in the market to seize.

13 Longevity and Brand Plays

Imagine a world in which people solve more problems with fewer things. The physical tools people use on a daily basis—from household appliances to clothing to furniture—have a useful life that can last generations instead of years. This takes the "design to last" philosophy to its extreme as high-quality products change hands through multiple owners and then leave a much smaller footprint when they finally reach the end of their useful lives.

In a paper published in *Current Opinion in Psychology* in 2021, two professors and a doctoral candidate at the Delft University of Technology in the Netherlands noted that consumers replace "31% of washing machines, 66% of vacuum cleaners, 56% of TVs and 69% of smartphones . . . for other reasons than being broken 'beyond' repair."[1] They cited several measures companies can undertake to reduce those numbers and increase the useful lives of products, including stimulating product care and maintenance, enabling upgradability, sustaining aesthetic value, and supporting the consumer's attachment to the product.

Companies pursuing that path have a much broader vocabulary than the word *replace*. They use *refurbish, resell, retain,* and *repair* instead. But they also recognize that this is an ecosystem challenge, not merely a product-design challenge. An ecosystem of shops or experts could keep products with a modular design up-to-date and in working order and maintain ongoing relationships with customers after the initial purchase. An active secondhand market can even reduce the need for new, lower-end products in a market as older products change hands when the needs of the original owner change.

The two companies we describe in the longevity play—the French retailer Fnac Darty and the US boot and fashion company Ariat—are creating value by implementing strategies aimed at making their own products or the products they sell have the longest and most valuable useful lives they can.

Longevity Play

When Fnac Darty announced a new strategic plan called "Everyday" in 2021, it launched several specific measures to support its stated mission to "commit to providing an educated choice and more sustainable consumption." These measures included the use of sustainability scores that help consumers select more durable and environmentally friendly products. Displayed clearly on the Fnac Darty website, these scores are derived from the company's proprietary after-sales repair database on the product reliability and the availability of spare parts.[2] "We opened our product durability data to be public," said Régis Koenig, the director of repair operations and durability at Fnac Darty. "We can compare the brands and build a database on that as we are in the quite unique position to have access to all this data."[3]

One major cornerstone of the Everyday initiative is the broader rollout of the company's subscription program for repairs, known as Darty Max. The basic program offers consumers a choice between three plans that include maintenance, unlimited repairs, free delivery and installation of new products, free return of old products, and an advisory service. The plans range in price from €11.99 to €21.99 ($13.19 to $24.19 in December 2023), depending on what appliances and devices the consumer wants to cover.[4] The ambition behind Darty Max is to "consolidate a high-quality long-term relationship with our customers and . . . to extend the lifespan of products." When the company announced the expansion, it aimed to have 2 million subscribers by 2025.[5] The subscription program generates recurring revenue for the company, which can also potentially charge higher prices as it follows the path from volume to value. "If we can convince our customers and also their customers that our products have a longer lifetime, they are eager to pay a little bit more," said Koenig.

Owing to life changes such as relocation, family status, or other factors, a consumer may want to replace an item that is still working. Fnac Darty can facilitate the resale of such products because its database and ongoing consumer relationships help it gauge a product's residual value. "In this scenario we know that the washing machine is working as we're the ones maintaining it and can therefore resell it knowing it's functional," Koenig said. Through 2022, the company reported that it had more than 800,000 Darty Max subscribers and had repaired more than 4 million products. The number of subscribers grew to more than one million by the end of third quarter in 2023.[6]

The US-based boot and apparel maker Ariat International doesn't have a subscription program like Darty Max, but it does offer ways for consumers to repair and resell the company's trademark cowboy boots and riding boots. It offers a repair program called NuShoe, which "brings your worn boots back to life, keeping them on your feet and out of landfills."[7] It has also launched Ariat Reboot, which is a peer-to-peer marketplace that connects buyers and sellers. The site allows customers to filter their search on the site by category, size, width, and condition, and it links the products to detailed product information in the Ariat catalog.[8] The company stresses the emotional attachment to the products, noting that "our boots are meant to live long lives. By reselling your boots, you're not just making a sale, you're connecting them to a new owner—someone who will be able to get every last bit of adventure out of them."[9]

The Demand Signals for the Longevity Play

By providing high-quality, long-lasting offerings, the longevity players address the image driven, the champions, the thoughtfuls, and, to some extent, the selectives. They also appeal to consumers following the "volume to value" trend.

The Simon-Kucher core studies revealed that consumers tend to use durability as a proxy for sustainability. Their logic makes sense. An efficient or durable product that does not require replacement or disposal is per se less wasteful than a comparable product with lower durability or a shorter lifespan. Even a product such as plastic LEGO bricks can be considered sustainable. They last so long that they are often passed down across generations rather than thrown away.

How Longevity Players Respond to the Demand Signals

The longevity play focuses on quality. It helps companies avoid the failure modes of "we can niche our way to success," "if it's green, it's good enough," and "it's only about the message."

It is one thing to produce a consistently high level of quality. But in the spirit of the new innovation paradigm success depends on how well longevity players communicate those benefits, how they create new business models to support the products over the course of their useful life, and how they reinforce the consumer's connection to the product. These challenges become more difficult in markets where consumer preferences change frequently.

Business models that support the longevity play include repair options, upgrade options, and secondhand markets. Products with timeless or modular design have a long first life, which consumers can extend by maintaining, repairing, refurbishing, or repurposing them. A product can also reach its second or third life through software and hardware changes. Software updates are suitable for phones, printers, speakers, and other electronics, while hardware upgrades are possible for products with a modular design.

This process can enhance loyalty by creating more consumer touchpoints within the company's ecosystem. They can apply their commercial creativity to develop engagement models—such as point systems, games, or subscriptions—to give consumers incentives to repair, refurbish, or resell a product instead of discarding it.

If the product becomes less relevant in one consumer's eyes, the existence of easily accessible and trustworthy secondhand markets allows them to find another pair of eyes for the product, thus extending its useful life. Andrea Baldo, the CEO of the high-end Danish fashion company GANNI, is confident that more and more consumers will buy into the secondhand model. "Our perception is that if you have to make the most sustainable choice, it is probably going to be a secondhand choice," he said. "We see a reduction into rental frequency, that's for sure, [but] we see secondhand booming more."[10]

Brand Play

Patagonia announced in 2022 that "the Earth is now our only shareholder."[11] Ownership of the company has transferred to Patagonia Purpose Trust and the nonprofit Holdfast Collective, which will distribute all profits as dividends to save the planet.

A brand born with sustainable ambitions and practices at its core, Patagonia has worked on numerous sustainable initiatives in its 50-year journey. Has it been worthwhile for the company to put environmental and social responsibility on equal footing with financial results?

The answer is yes.

Patagonia is recognized as the sustainable champion in the outdoor-clothing industry. It has earned the US Secretary of State's Award for Corporate Excellence in Climate Innovation, and the United Nations awarded Patagonia its flagship environmental honor for entrepreneurial vision. This valuable positioning as a leader in sustainability decreases customer-acquisition costs because Patagonia is top-of-mind for consumers and has built a sense of community among consumers, who see it as a way to enhance their own personal brands. Patagonia products have become fashion staples in the Wall Street and Silicon Valley communities.

Patagonia has undertaken what we call a brand play. The goal of a brand play is to "own" the sustainability positioning and to act as the sustainable market leader, as in how Volvo is historically perceived as "synonymous with safety" and once owned that brand positioning in the automotive industry.[12] A strong brand purpose not only lowers acquisition costs but also increases loyalty and advocacy and makes brands more valuable. "Brands for which consumers perceive a strong brand purpose grew their value by 175%—more than double that of brands perceived by consumers as having a weaker purpose," according to Kantar, which analyzed brand-value growth across a 12-year period.[13]

Evangelist players take the brand play to its extreme by matching their sustainable commitments with financial commitments. They bring purpose and profit into full harmony. Evangelist players usually commit themselves either to donate a percentage of sales or profit to environmental purposes or to reinvest the bulk of their earnings with the sole purpose of accelerating their own sustainability transformation. The latter companies aggressively sacrifice current earnings for future profits. It is easier for privately held or family-owned companies to become evangelist players and take greater risks because they do not have the stringent reporting requirements and distribution obligations that publicly traded companies have. So although this extreme version of a brand play offers privately held or family-owned companies a vast opportunity to disrupt an industry, it constitutes an enormous risk for publicly traded companies.

The Demand Signals for the Brand Play

The brand play caters to consumer archetypes positioned higher up the vertical axis in our segmentation model in figure 6.1: the image driven, the champions, the thoughtfuls, and, to some extent, the selectives. Some forms of the brand play address planet savers. The brand players also appeal to consumers who are part of the "silent to vocal" trend we described in chapter 2.

Companies cannot help consumers to take an active role in sustainability and build their own personal brands or image when consumers themselves have no idea how much of a difference they are making. The target archetypes for a brand play express a greater need for knowledge and trust, a need reinforced by the existence of greenwashing. Brand players rely on genuine and transparent communication to overcome those barriers and earn consumers' trust.

The brand play will appeal to consumers who want to buy products from sustainable brands that they wish to be associated with. Wearing Patagonia, for example, helps consumers feel they share similar values and purpose. When companies use a strong brand and intensive genuine communication to scale rapidly, those assets and capabilities can help them differentiate themselves and potentially earn a premium when the mere presence of sustainable features is no longer a differentiator.

How Brand Players Respond to the Demand Signals

Brand players incorporate sustainability as the core of their corporate strategy and make it the organizing principle of all their activities. They know that actions such as launching an eco-friendly product line and complying with ESG regulations are important but not sufficient to achieve their grander purpose. This awareness helps them avoid failure modes such as "we can niche our way to success," "it's only about the message," and "winning the compliance game."

The shoes, accessories, and apparel company TOMS practices genuine and transparent communication to strengthen its brand. Consumers around the world realize quickly that the entire company centers itself around ecological and social sustainability principles and practices. Since its inception, TOMS has reported and communicated about production and manufacturing processes and social responsibility partnerships and has answered consumers' questions with the same genuine and transparent approach.[14]

The expanded consumer relationship generated through increased loyalty and advocacy creates opportunities for brand players to become trusted sustainability advisers. They can redefine and elevate consumer expectations about how sustainable companies should behave and communicate, and the higher they move the bar, the more they increase the distance between themselves and competitors. Expanding knowledge is another positive experience for consumers that can heighten their awareness and motivate them to seek out even more ways to act sustainably, while enhancing their view of their trusted brand.

14 Mass Affordability and Antiwaste Plays

Imagine a world in which as many people as possible have access to sustainable solutions, use them efficiently, and leave behind the smallest possible trace in their use. Think of liquid products from beverages to cleaning products. Is it more efficient for companies to add water at a factory and ship heavy bottles long distances or for consumers to add water to concentrates in their own homes? In the spirit of creative destruction, is it more sustainable and more profitable to eliminate the "liquid" from liquid detergent entirely and offer an alternative such as laundry sheets?

These questions highlight the inherent tension in achieving mass affordability and eliminating waste. But that tension is more complex than it appears at first glance. One challenge with mass affordability—and the mass production that underpins it—is the balance a company needs to strike between the technological push on the supply side and the needs of consumers on the demand side. "The profit lure of mass production obviously has a place in the plans and strategy of business management, but it must always *follow* hard thinking about the customer," said Theodore Levitt in his landmark article "Marketing Myopia" in 1975.[1]

Waste, meanwhile, is much more than physical waste. When we discussed the introduction of laundry sheets in chapter 11, we mentioned how much plastic packaging ends up in landfills in the United States. But waste also concerns economic efficiency, as Marco Bertini and Oded Koenigsberg point out in their book *The Ends Game: How*

Smart Companies Stop Selling Products and Start Delivering Value. They define three types of waste. *Access waste* occurs when the customer cannot readily obtain the means necessary to achieve a desirable outcome. *Consumption waste* occurs when an asset—a car, an apartment, a bicycle, a printer, a medical device—sits idle for a large portion of its useful life. It also occurs when consumers do not acquire an asset in the first place because they believe that the expected use does not justify committing to ownership. *Performance waste* occurs if "the product or service doesn't deliver the value expected from it."[2]

The plays we introduced in chapter 13 included sustainability as a complementary factor to brand and quality, two of the traditional value drivers. In the two plays described in this chapter, price plays a more prominent role.

Mass Affordability Play

This play requires a relentless emphasis on lower costs and greater scale without imposing a quality penalty on consumers. Achieving both lower costs and greater scale is a test for a company's entire ecosystem, from its suppliers to its labor force to the infrastructure that supports the sustainable solution after the sale.

The consumers in several archetypes made it clear not only that they are unwilling to pay a premium for the mere presence of a sustainable feature but also that price is a major value driver behind most of their day-to-day purchase decisions.

In a blog post in 2013, Elon Musk stressed the idea of mass affordability in Tesla's mission at the time: "Our goal when we created Tesla a decade ago was the same as it is today: to accelerate the advent of sustainable transport by bringing compelling mass market electric cars to market as soon as possible."[3] That mission is now broader, as Tesla is aiming to "accelerate the transition to renewable energy. Our masterplan has set a clear pathway to achieve that mission: the transformation of cost-intensive small-series products to cheaper mass-series vehicles."[4]

Several factors have accelerated Tesla's success and secured its first-mover advantage over other EV manufacturers. First, the company has been rethinking the entire production process of cars to reduce cost. At its Investor Day in March 2023, Tesla announced a parallel and serial assembly approach, in contrast to the classic sequential line. The new approach could improve efficiency by 30 percent, contributing to lower costs.[5] Second, in contrast to most car manufacturers, Tesla owns most of its value chain. It operates with a direct-sales business model, offering sales online without traditional dealers. This model gives it more flexibility in terms of operating margin because it has lower operating expenses.[6] Third, Tesla's charging-network infrastructure, built around its patented superchargers, has become a standard in many markets.[7] These factors allowed Tesla to scale up its production and operations globally to become one of the first EVs to reach a critical mass of vehicles sold.[8] The company's relentless pursuit of cost savings is changing the automotive industry at its core and exemplifies how a single company can use a mass affordability play to influence the structure of an entire industry.

Tesla cars originally came with premium prices, but the firm aims to capture the mass market and thereby increase the number of consumers to support the company's mission. The higher volumes will also help the company continue to improve its economies of scale. The company has recently reduced prices across several regions to make its cars more affordable. In late 2023, speculation started that Tesla would produce an EV priced at €25,000 ($27,500 in December 2023), a fraction of the prevailing average price of an EV in Europe, €65,000 ($71,500).[9] It would build the vehicles at a German factory near Berlin, according to reports. Lower operating costs would help the company still make healthy margins on vehicles despite the lower prices.

The Demand Signals for the Mass Affordability Play

Mass affordability players work to mitigate or eliminate price as a major barrier to adoption of sustainable products. It appeals to all consumer archetypes but will resonate most with the skeptics, the cost conscious, and the planet savers. Lower prices may even provide incentives to encourage nonbelievers to buy the product, though not necessarily for its sustainable features. Tesla has obviously recognized this barrier as well as the contrast between willingness to pay and ability to pay. "The desire for people to own a Tesla is extremely high," Musk has said. "The limiting factor is their ability to pay for a Tesla."[10]

How Mass Affordability Players Respond to the Demand Signals

In line with a penetration strategy, mass affordability players aim to use lower prices as their primary means to achieve rapid scale for their sustainable products. They can also create barriers to entry if they can scale so quickly that it becomes impractical or prohibitively expensive for second movers to enter the market with competitively priced products.

This leads us back to the new innovation paradigm described in detail in chapter 11. Do lower prices come with sustainable products that are otherwise superior to or are on par with or have trade-offs compared to the competitive nonsustainable products? All else held equal, superior sustainable products at affordable prices will win the greater market share. Producing superior or even on-par products at affordable prices may sound like an obvious objective to aim for, but it usually requires a high degree of commercial creativity and—for incumbents and rapidly evolving sustainability natives—a strategy for creative destruction.

Disruptive innovation, a term coined by Clayton Christensen, describes a process by which a product or service takes root initially in simple applications at the bottom of a market and then relentlessly moves up market, eventually displacing established competitors.[11] This approach offers a shorter way to mass affordability, with products stripped down to their core still offering a differentiated sustainable benefit at an affordable price. However, this process needs to be followed with caution to avoid the "if it's green, it's good enough" failure mode. A careful understanding of consumer value drivers and trade-offs for each consumer archetype is necessary to limit the high risks of stripping out features that consumers may perceive as important or essential.

Recall that Tesla presents another route to the mass affordability play. The company produced a high-end, sustainable alternative and used the profits from early adopters to invest in its longer-term play of reaching mass affordability. Tesla was not an overnight success. The route it took is longer because offering sustainable products at affordable prices requires companies to redesign their business model to bring down production costs and sell at scale. Tesla's path thus has some similarities to a classic innovation approach rather than the new innovation paradigm. Companies trying to emulate the former path today, however, will have far less time to let the traditional process unfold.

The combined challenge of commercial creativity and creative destruction for incumbents can arise when an innovative product significantly reduces some revenue streams or eliminates the factors that powered them. Kodak faced that challenge in its mass-market film business, and automotive OEMs may experience it with their service business at dealerships. Dealers generate a great deal of revenue and profit from service, but EVs require minimal or no service. How can dealers or the OEM make up those shortfalls?

Tesla may be showing those OEMs the way by creating supplementary revenue sources. It launched Tesla Insurance because it felt that insurance companies charged excessive premiums for EVs. The new business not only generates revenue but also provides Tesla with additional data it can use to improve product development. The insurance, offered mainly in the United States, charges its premium using a SafetyScore based on real-time driving behavior monitored by existing technology within EVs.[12] Bringing insurance in-house is another way that Tesla can manage and lower the total cost of ownership for its vehicles.

Antiwaste Play

"By the time you finish reading this page, another 5 million single-use plastic bottles will be sold around the world."

That message appears at the top of a page on the website of Soda-Stream, a company that offers at-home carbonation for water and a wide variety of flavored drinks. Data back up the claim. More than a million single-use plastic bottles are sold worldwide every minute, but only 9 percent of that plastic has been recycled. In contrast, 79 percent has ended up in landfills or the natural environment.[13]

SodaStream is an antiwaste player that demonstrates that sustainability does not require sacrifices in product quality or choice. Designed to last for three years, each SodaStream bottle replaces thousands of single-use plastic bottles. The company also offers exchangeable CO_2 cylinders to encourage reuse and eliminate waste. The company has pledged to save up to 76 billion single-use plastic bottles by 2025 in line with its vision of eliminating single-use plastic waste and promoting sustainability.[14]

The Demand Signals for the Antiwaste Play

The antiwaste play has a universal appeal because all eight consumer archetypes—even nonbelievers—have some distaste for waste. Companies can reduce or eliminate waste with programs for re- and upcycling, minimized packaging, and better product customization. But consumers also have a personal role to play, as the Canadian journalist J. B. MacKinnon asserts in his book *The Day the World Stops Shopping— How Ending Consumerism Saves the Environment and Ourselves*. Many companies build their business models around the excessive shopping of consumers, who find their habits of overconsumption hard to break.[15]

Recall our conversation with Lisa, a planet saver, who uses the term *mind-boggling* to describe the apparent selfishness of people who are unwilling to rethink their consumption habits. She reflects the growing trend "from excess waste to antiwaste" that we described in part I (see figure 4.2). But many of the other trends stemming from the consumer pull for sustainable solutions have elements of efficiency and waste reduction embedded in them. The "from atomistic to holistic" trend reduces steps in a supply chain, "from linear to circular" reduces the use of virgin materials, and "individual to shared economy" helps shift consumer habits from ownership to reuse.

The frustration with waste has led to changes in consumption patterns for many consumers, with some reducing their overall consumption in meaningful ways. However, companies can help guide these behavioral changes by adopting an antiwaste play. Products designed and promoted from an antiwaste principle help consumers understand whether a product is sustainable and trust that fact. They may also offer lower prices due to a company's own savings from efficiencies, better material choices, and changes to its business model. Many of the focus-group participants expressed this intuitive logic, noting that less wasteful and more efficient production processes should lead directly to lower prices and great access for consumers.

How Antiwaste Players Respond to the Demand Signals

The antiwaste play needs to offer real solutions, which means companies must avoid the "it's only about the message" failure mode. SodaStream invented a disruptive new product that reinforces the achievement of waste reduction every time a consumer uses it. But it has tapped only one of many opportunities to find lucrative ways to create a positive user experience and eliminate waste at the same time.

Other companies are currently working on adapting their business models to fit with antiwaste principles, such as participating in extended ecosystems that use a circular approach to minimize both waste and the current overuse of virgin materials. McDonald's supplies Ford Motor Company with coffee chaff, the dried skin of the bean, which Ford converts into materials used in the production of vehicle parts. Adidas partners with Parley for Oceans by using ocean plastic waste to make its "Parley" collection of shoes and clothing. "Through our collaboration with Parley for the Oceans, we want to inspire and mobilize an entire generation to help shape the future of our planet," adidas states. "We're on a mission to help end plastic waste. And this is a fight we can't lose."[16]

The success of many circular ventures depends on consumer participation because recycled and upcycled materials have become a scarce resource. One approach is to incentivize consumers to engage. Many

US states and countries around the world have the classic deposit-and-return system for bottles. Producers add an additional cost—a deposit—that consumers can claim back if they return the empty plastic bottles. The monetary incentive is rather insignificant compared to the total price paid, but the programs work. Denmark implemented its program in 2002 and achieved a return rate of 93 percent in 2021.[17] The Madewell Denim Recycling Program incentivizes consumers to recycle and upcycle materials. It encourages consumers to bring in their old jeans, regardless of the brand, in exchange for a $20 credit toward a new pair of Madewell jeans. Madewell collaborates with Blue Jeans Go Green and Habitat for Humanity to convert the old jeans into insulation for houses. Since the program's inception, it has successfully recycled more than 520,000 pairs of jeans and insulated more than 690 homes.[18] These incentive structures serve as effective nudges for consumers motivated by a strong sense of responsibility.

The antiwaste play can also encompass the usage of less material to begin with. Examples include minimized packaging as well as meal kits designed to reduce food waste. Too Good to Go is an innovative mobile application that aims to combat food waste. It works by connecting customers with restaurants, bakeries, supermarkets, and other food-related businesses that have surplus food at the end of the day. Businesses can sell their leftover food at a significantly reduced price to Too Good to Go users instead of throwing it out.[19] Other companies, such as Misfit Market, combat food-waste issues by making cosmetically challenged food available to consumers at affordable prices.

Waste is inherently unsustainable and eternally frustrating for consumers. The antiwaste play offers companies a chance to give their commercial creativity free rein to attract consumers, solve problems for them beyond waste, reduce their frustrations, and create a growing revenue stream.

15   Ease-of-Choice and Engagement Plays

Imagine a world in which feeling good about doing good isn't merely an abstract principle or aspiration but a practical part of day-to-day life. Instead of being asked to pay extra to help an airline invest in sustainable aviation fuel, for example, you pay a specific amount to offset CO_2 and earn additional miles, points, or discounts. What if you had a sustainability account in your city or town—similar to a points systems on a credit card—that gave you credits for recycling, composting, cleaning up, or other sustainable activities?

These personal-rewards systems are becoming increasingly common in areas from auto insurance to online shopping. An article in the *Asian Journal of Business Ethics* cites numerous studies that show that "gamification"—the use of games, contests, and other reward mechanisms in consumer interactions—can encourage behaviors and make shopping fun and attractive by increasing motivation, engagement, and loyalty.[1] Instead of making a claim that is hard for a consumer to validate, such as the planting of trees or the saving of polar bears if a consumer buys a product, these games offer a mix of immediate and postponed gratification as consumers watch their points or credits accumulate and then have the pleasure of redeeming them.

Companies can make it much easier for consumers to find the sustainable solutions they want by framing the choices more attractively or actively engaging consumers before, during, and after their purchase experience. That advice leads to our final two plays.

Ease-of-Choice Play

If someone were to ask you to make a list of all the products that you associate strongly with sustainability, how long would they have to wait before you added "sausage" to the list?

For the German food manufacturer Rügenwalder Mühle, combining "sausage" and "sustainability" is not a contradiction. It has been a way of life and a business philosophy for the family-owned company in one way or another since its founding in 1834. Known for its craftmanship and high-quality ingredients, the company has long ranked as a market leader in sausages and hams. Then it launched vegetarian and vegan alternatives in 2014, becoming one of the first movers of the products in the German market. The move proved so popular that seven years later Rügenwalder Mühle was generating more sales from meat alternatives than from meat products for the first time in its history.[2]

Rügenwalder Mühle scaled its vegan and vegetarian business so quickly because it is an ease-of-choice player. Its vision is an ideal expression of what it means to remove the barriers to access that consumers face: "We want everyone to be able to eat healthily and sustainably in an uncomplicated way—without restrictions and compromises in taste and enjoyment." It applies the same focus and commitment to its sourcing activities and its general operations, with the purpose of "not acting today at the expense of tomorrow."[3]

The way Rügenwalder Mühle communicates with consumers is coherent and consistent, whether in stores or on its website. The company uses its power as a traditional leading brand to make its non-meat products easily available and accessible by placing them next to its meat products in stores, which enables all consumers to make their choices at the shelf rather than searching for a special section or shelf in the store to find what they want. The company builds its website in the same way, viewing its consumers as hungry people who want great taste rather than creating a perceived imbalance in favor of meat eaters and against vegans and vegetarians. Its communication around the brand also reinforces trust by emphasizing the other steps the company takes to act sustainably, such as the use of recycled packaging.

The Demand Signals for the Ease-of-Choice Play

Ease-of-choice players address the accessibility, trust, and knowledge barriers that consumers must hurdle. They create awareness of sustainable alternatives and then make it easy for the consumer to understand, find, and choose the sustainable alternatives when they purchase. Accessibility is especially relevant for the image driven and the champion, and it is important to the selectives and the thoughtfuls.

Trust and knowledge are chronic sources of frustration for many consumer archetypes. Consumers see or hear that a company has made a commitment to sustainability, but then they find that sustainability is little more than a marketing gimmick unless the consumer benefit is clear. Customers can experience and perceive the difference. A positive consumption experience is the best evidence of whether those commitments are genuine, but before consumers even purchase the product, they need a minimum level of trust in those claims.

Our focus groups and subsequent interviews showed that consumers tend to spend more time researching sustainable solutions, often because they do not trust the available information currently provided by companies or on products. They strive to make educated decisions and often use durability and quality as proxies for sustainability. But it remains nearly impossible for any consumer to fully vet everything they consume unless they make that research their life's work.

How Ease-of-Choice Players Respond to the Demand Signals

Would you buy a crownless pineapple rather than a crowned one if you have the option? Researchers placed crownless and crowned pineapples next to each other in an independent retail store, with the crownless pineapples priced two cents lower. Over a couple of weeks, the results showed that consumers bought just as many crownless as crowned pineapples when the communication highlighted the environmental benefits associated with crownless pineapples. Removing the crowns from pineapples reduces carbon emissions and labor costs because the crownless fruit is more economical to pack, ship, store, and stock.[4]

The side-by-side presentation of the pineapples made the choice for consumers easier not only because of the clear visible cues but also because of the opportunity to explain the benefits clearly with both emotional appeals and rational appeals at the point of sale.[5] The same form of presentation can apply to plastic packaging versus naturally colored cardboard boxes, allowing the consumer to process several cues and pieces of information at the shelf. E-commerce sites such as booking.com have begun to include the keyword *sustainability* as a search filter, which is another way that companies can make it easier for consumers to choose.

Nonetheless, the many complexities and parameters of answering basic questions and challenging claims on sustainability leave many consumers frustrated. They are left to untangle a web of well-intentioned labels that end up creating confusion instead of clarity. Having standard formats for product labeling and presentation could make it easier for consumers to make the choices they want to make.

Recall in chapter 2 when we mentioned how carbon labels should become as ubiquitous as detailed nutrition labels on food products at the grocery store. Assessing the overall impact of a purchase can be complicated. Simply drinking a glass of milk can leave consumers conflicted. Is it environmentally better—and more sustainable—to drink almond milk or dairy milk? The question is open to debate, and that is precisely the problem. Imagine that someone decides to stop drinking dairy milk because dairy herds produce greenhouse gases. They decide to drink almond milk instead, but without realizing that they may have traded one form of potential environmental harm for another. The production of almonds in California reportedly consumes 10 percent of the state's water supply at a time when the state is in the midst of a severe drought. One scientist estimates that the soil in California in the early 2000s had not been so dry in more than 400 years.[6] At the same time, the accusations that almonds draw down too much water do not mention how much water goes into the production of dairy milk.

Knowing whether they have made a difference is important to consumers, who often don't realize the dilemmas they face. We currently lack a common language to help consumers make informed decisions about whether they and the companies they buy from are living up to their sustainability commitments. Most people probably know their weight and may even have an ideal weight goal, for example. But few people know their carbon footprint, never mind what actions contribute to it and what their ideal should be. Do you?

With this complication in mind, the use of standardization and easy comparisons creates additional opportunities for accelerating the growth in the development of sustainable products. Companies can design product versions along sustainability attributes and offer "good–better–best" value propositions because consumers have the confidence and trust to evaluate the differences between good, better, and best.

The Danish Animal Welfare Label on Milk (Dyrevelfærdsmærket på Mælk), introduced by the Danish Veterinary and Food Administration (Fødevarestyrelsen), has seen widespread adoption by companies including Arla, a leading Danish dairy corporation. The label uses a three-level system of heart symbols to represent good, better, and best standards of animal welfare in production. The labels facilitate ease of choice by allowing consumers to quickly evaluate products based on these standards. A YouGov survey commissioned by the Danish Veterinary and Food Administration in 2022 revealed that seven out of ten Danes consider animal welfare when purchasing food and that more than 70 percent were familiar with and trusted the Animal Welfare Label.[7]

Engagement Play

The LEGO Group could exemplify any of the six strategic plays, but what really stands out is the company's level of engagement with its consumers. It has embedded that idea in its mission statement, which is to "inspire and develop the builders of tomorrow."[8] That mission is a two-way street, though, because those builders are also inspiring and developing the LEGO Group of tomorrow. "Kids are inspiring us to be more sustainable," said Tim Brooks, the vice president and global head of sustainability at the LEGO Group, as he talked about the letters the company receives. "They want us to be more ambitious and do more."[9]

The LEGO Group places an emphasis on nurturing a community of consumers instead of simply selling them bags of bricks to play with. It also integrates them into the development and refinement of the company's products, packaging, and go-to-market strategy. The recent transition from plastic bags to paper prepack bags, for example, came to fruition through user input. The company will phase out single-use plastic bags gradually over the next three years, and the paper-based bags "can be recycled in many of our markets."[10] "[The] paper prepack bag was elevated and accelerated through that pressure from kids, I think is fair to say," Brooks said. "During the development, we also discovered that kids found it hard to open the plastic bags," he added. "That was a moment where we realized that we could deliver something for kids that was better."

The new paper bags are easier to open, are recyclable, and can assist in the building process because the company can print symbols, numbers, and instructions on them. The transition shows how an effort to become more sustainable can yield an approach that is "sustainable and superior" in the spirit of the scenarios we described in chapter 11. "It is obvious that when you look at something with green lenses, you also get consumer benefits," Brooks said.

The growth of the secondhand market for LEGO bricks also has its roots in the engaged user community. In 2000, a LEGO fan named Dan Jezek founded a company called BrickBay, which later became Brick-Link, to facilitate the exchange of ideas in the LEGO community and to connect individual buyers and sellers of LEGO bricks. In 2019, the company formally became part of the LEGO Group and currently has more than 10,000 sellers and more than one million registered members in more than 70 countries.[11]

The LEGO Group also has the Replay program, which accepts submissions of used bricks, cleans and sorts them, and donates them.

"We're donating those bricks to good causes," said Tim Brooks. Through organizations such as the Boys and Girls Clubs of America, Teach for America, and Indigenous Canadian charities, they reach children who generally "don't have access to learning through play."

In chapter 10, we described how durability and backward compatibility help the LEGO Group build the basis for a sustainable business, even though the company manufactures its bricks from the petroleum-based plastic ABS.[12] "Durability is a double-edged sword," Brooks explained. LEGO products can last for decades, but that durability is "hard to achieve with more sustainable materials, so we need to also think of durability as a sustainability trait in itself." Replacing ABS with another material could compel the LEGO Group to extract a quality penalty either by reducing the bricks' in-play performance or reducing their durability. It could also lead to a price premium due to the additional upfront development costs.

But the company is consciously avoiding both paths. "You want to ensure plastic doesn't go to waste and doesn't enter the nature stream," Brooks said. "But we need high-performing materials, and at the moment recycled materials are not always in that category of high-performing and safe materials." In October 2023, the company abandoned some plans to use recycled plastic materials for bricks when it learned that the process would lead to higher carbon emissions.[13] Another alternative is to use biobased plastics, which the LEGO Group attempts with processed sugar cane sourced from Brazil. Biobased plastics "are now at least one of those elements in 50 percent of boxes," Brooks said. "But the goal, the success of the project, the success of what we're trying to do, is change the entire portfolio, not change 5 percent of the portfolio."

Comparing the challenge of substituting biobased materials for ABS to trying to make a bicycle out of wood, Brooks stressed that it is difficult to find an alternative to ABS. "It is clear that we need to find better ABS rather than finding new materials that can do the job of ABS," he said. Regarding the implementation of a price premium, Brooks stressed that "consumers don't want to pay more, and we think that they shouldn't have to pay more."

The Demand Signals for the Engagement Play

Similar to ease of choice, the engagement play aims to overcome the barriers of accessibility, trust, and knowledge. But it relies more heavily on creating positive consumer experiences and incentivizing consumers to engage in acting more sustainably. It appeals to the motivators around feeling good, social recognition, and social pressure. Companies can use the engagement play to attract and retain the image driven and selectives, who give relatively high weight to social motivators. It is also relevant for the skeptics, cost conscious, and planet savers because it builds on greater knowledge and trust.

The engagement play also addresses consumers who are following the "from silent to vocal" trend. An undercurrent throughout part III is the urge among many consumers to become advocates, either to amplify their own positive experience or to let other consumers benefit from the research they have done. The community element in the engagement play fits well to this context as sustainability has become more personal for consumers than ever before.

How Engagement Players Respond to the Demand Signals

Engagement players avoid the "if it's green it's good enough" failure mode by always looking for ways to go above and beyond. They also rely on incentives to motivate and engage consumers.

Many airlines now offer consumers the opportunity to pay an additional fee to offset their CO_2 consumption. CEO Michael O'Leary of Ryanair, however, has said that only 1 percent of his passengers pay the fee of €2.00 ($2.20 as of December 2023) to offset flight emissions. This aligns with results from a study by the Air Transport Action Group, which found that uptake of voluntary carbon emission offsets was only between 1 and 3 percent of flights.[14]

The question is whether these low levels of uptake reflect fundamental refusal, disinterest, or a lack of engagement. In the latter case, the right incentives can help improve the results. The Nobel Prize–winning economist Richard Thaler draws a distinction between "nudges," or actions that positively influence behavior, and "sludges," or actions

Archetype	Strategic Play					
	Brand	Longevity	Mass Affordability	Ease-of-Choice	Engagement	Antiwaste
Champions 8%	✓	✓		✓		✓
Thoughtfuls 9%	✓	✓		✓		✓
Planet Savers 13%	✓	✓	✓			✓
Image Driven 10%	✓	✓		✓	✓	
Selectives 8%	✓	✓	✓	✓	✓	✓
Cost Conscious 18%			✓		✓	✓
Skeptics 19%			✓	✓	✓	✓
Nonbelievers 15%			✓			✓

Main commercial levers implicated: Price   Communication   Offering

Figure 15.1
How the strategic plays align with the eight consumer archetypes.

that either "discourage behavior that is in a person's best interest [or] encourage self-defeating behavior."[15] Companies can also use contests or game elements to increase engagement. Lunar, a Danish neobank that collaborates with organizations that clean the oceans, employs that tactic. With a Project Blue Membership, a consumer can decide how much they wish to donate for every 1,000 Danish Kroner they spend on their credit card. An app tracks and visualizes how much plastic the donation has helped remove from the oceans.

In the engagement play, companies can also use consumer communities to foster engagement, just as Patagonia, a brand player, fostered a community on Wall Street and in Silicon Valley, where the brand has become a corporate wardrobe staple.

*   *   *

These six strategic plays are the ones we have identified to be the most successful in winning over consumers. Companies need to make a full commitment to whatever play or combination of plays they select. They cannot engage in any of these plays half-heartedly. Each play caters to one or more of the archetypes presented in part III. Based on the primary barriers perceived by the different archetypes and the main commercial levers implicated in each play, we have matched the archetypes and strategic plays to each other in figure 15.1.

Transformative megatrends are powerful and dominating by nature. They redraw industry boundaries as companies diversify outside their primary sector. But megatrends are also linked to vast amounts of value creation. Past megatrends have ignited growth by creating new business opportunities, greater efficiency and productivity, and continued reinvestment. The sustainability megatrend is just starting to create these opportunities and—just as digitalization did—will create more and more opportunities that are currently beyond our collective imagination.

Epilogue: Detours and High-Speed Lanes

Where is the demand revolution heading?

The consumer-driven pull that sustainability has created will change every industry and business in the coming decades. Like every transformative megatrend before it, sustainability will see the demise of established industry leaders and the emergence of new elite companies. As noted earlier, Bill Gates believes that sustainability will spawn "eight Teslas, 10 Teslas" as well as additional "Microsoft, Google, Amazon-type companies" as it unfolds.[1] That represents trillions of dollars in market capitalization for companies no one has even heard of yet.

Several factors beyond the direct control of companies and consumers will influence the speed and magnitude of these changes. Some could throw off companies' plans, while others may accelerate progress and lead to exponential growth even sooner. We refer to the former as *detours* and to the latter as *high-speed lanes* and highlight a few of them in this epilogue.

Natural Disasters and Socioeconomic Shocks

Natural disasters are making environmental sustainability an up-close-and-personal issue for many of the world's consumers. Whether it is flooding in Germany, wildfires in California, or hurricanes in Florida, every increase in the intensity, frequency, or breadth of these events heightens the urgency that consumers feel to make lifestyle changes.

Inflation also affects consumer spending on sustainable solutions. In our 2022 core study, one-third of European and North American respondents said they were less likely to buy sustainable goods and services because of inflation, and 30% said they were more selective in which categories they would pay for sustainable alternatives because of inflation.[2] But we warn once again about conflating willingness to pay and ability to pay. This reluctance does not signal diminished interest in sustainability but rather a trend that makes the solutions that consumers desire less affordable.

Supply-Side and Technological Disruptions

The sustainability megatrend will not have exclusive rights to change the course of the world in the coming years. Technological breakthroughs in battery technology, materials science, carbon capture, and other fields will open up new and unforeseen opportunities to create value. At the same time, a rapid increase in demand for sustainability-related materials could lead to shortages or persistent supply disruptions. The US Department of Energy reported that "private sector investments in American-made battery technologies have been increasing over the last few years, with 208 as of September 2023." The federal government had also announced 27 investments. The department estimates that "the more than $100 billion in investments (private and federal) will create over 75,000 jobs."[3]

Other technological advancements could emerge as a high-speed lane or a detour. Generative artificial intelligence (AI) has already arrived. In two months after ChatGPT's launch at the end of November 2022, it had 100 million monthly active users. It took Instagram two and a half years and TikTok nine months to get to the same position.[4] AI's influence on business and private lives may continue to grow over decades, but it will also have environmental consequences that could slow its progress. AI is responsible for a large carbon footprint. MIT reported in March 2023 that "the cloud now has a larger carbon footprint than the entire airline industry, and a single data center might consume an amount of electricity equivalent to 50,000 homes. . . . Training just one AI model can emit more than 626,000 pounds of carbon dioxide equivalent—which is nearly five times the lifetime emissions of an average American car."[5] AI initiatives will also compete with sustainability initiatives for attention and investment from consumers, companies, governments, and media, which may potentially slow down the acceleration of the sustainability megatrend.

A new transformative megatrend may supersede digitalization in the coming decades if quantum computing becomes commercially relevant, which may happen within the next decade. An article in the *MIT Sloan Management Review* in early 2023 described the significant economic advantages that quantum computing could generate, including its ability to solve complex optimization problems much more quickly and to accelerate research and development processes.[6]

Government Regulation and Intervention

Many consumers feel like they cannot fight the sustainability problem alone, and many have their doubts that companies will make a serious effort. That is where governments can step in with mixtures of regulations, tariffs, subsidies, and other incentives to steer corporate and consumer behavior. We are neither advocating nor forecasting *what* will happen but rather noting that significant government intervention will always be creating new detours and high-speed lanes.

The European Union has implemented a range of directives and regulations such as the Corporate Sustainability Reporting Directive, a part of the European Green Deal, and is setting out new, extensive requirements for companies to report sustainability information, including their emissions. Companies will have to apply the new rules for the first time in the 2024 financial year for reports published in 2025.[7] Such regulations will move entire industries toward more sustainable practices, but they also pose the risk that companies will slip into failure modes by trading off competitive advantage in search of compliance advantages.

Activist Shareholders

Investors, employees, and the media all have a part to play in driving forward the sustainability megatrend. Will they lead or follow as the trend evolves?

When Shell Oil reported record-breaking profits of $40 billion for 2022, the company's allegedly unsatisfactory efforts in implementing an energy-transition strategy became a dealbreaker for some shareholders. The environmental law firm ClientEarth, in its capacity as a shareholder, filed a lawsuit against Shell's board in the High Court of England and Wales in February 2023. According to one report, "Shell's directors are being personally sued for allegedly failing to adequately manage the risks associated with the climate emergency in a first-of-its-kind lawsuit that could have widespread implications for how other companies plan to cut emissions." "We do not accept ClientEarth's allegations," a Shell spokesman said in response.[8]

Unilever came under pressure from activist shareholders in 2022 for apparently heading too far in the opposite direction. One large shareholder "accused the company of neglecting business fundamentals while overemphasizing its commitment to climate and social causes."[9] In chapter 13, we mentioned that privately held or family-owned companies can sometimes place bigger bets with a longer payback horizon because they do not have the stringent reporting requirements and distribution obligations that publicly traded companies have.

Colliding Megatrends

The transformative megatrend of globalization has made the world more interconnected than ever before, but it also leaves the world more vulnerable and exposed to risks that follow international instability and disruptions. The collision of sustainability and globalization creates tensions between finding more efficient ways for companies to ship goods over long distances and finding ways to produce goods closer to their markets.

The transformative megatrend of digitalization, meanwhile, continues unabated after more than 25 years. It is still introducing new changes as others mature. Generation Z and many millennials have never known a world without the commercial internet and smartphones. The next generation will never know a world without streaming media options, hybrid modes of work, touchless commerce, and many other digital aspects of day-to-day life.

The collision of digitalization and sustainability seems to hold greater promise than the collision with globalization. Peter Weckesser, chief digital officer at Schneider Electric, said at the World Economic Forum annual meeting in 2022 that "most sustainability challenges are inherently complex. They demand new thinking, actionable insights, scalable solutions, and expert partnership to drive change at a systemic level. This is where digitalization becomes an imperative."[10] These two megatrends have a likelihood of not only coexisting but also codeveloping to become a source of disruptive new innovations that will accelerate the speed of sustainable transition for companies and consumers in a market as well as for entire sectors and economies.

The collision of sustainability with a quantum revolution could be game changing for the speed and scale that the new innovation paradigm requires. The article in the *MIT Sloan Management Review* mentioned earlier also speculates that quantum computing could cut research-and-development times by an order of magnitude in some industries.[11] These collisions and the resulting convergence may be the ultimate source of exponential growth that allows the sustainability megatrend to follow the path of previous transformative megatrends and improve the lives of billions of people.

To borrow a word from CFO John Lawler at Ford, there's going to be some "bumpiness" as business leaders leave behind the constraints of the green mirage and embrace the demand revolution.[12] But these bumps will not halt the progress of the sustainability megatrend.

Acknowledgments

Just as we have delved into sustainability transformations in *The Demand Revolution*, a book reflects the collective contributions of many individuals, each fulfilling vital roles.

We give a special thanks to Frank Luby, who has spent countless hours with us providing insightful inputs, debating ideas, and improving concepts and content. We also owe a special thanks to our colleague from Simon-Kucher, Rebecca Cecilie Møller, who assisted us in conducting the essential research and extensive analyses this book relies on. We also very much appreciate the support we received from Daniel Vámosi Snell, who served as our shadow editor and provided us with continuous reviews and invaluable feedback.

Our colleagues at Simon-Kucher challenged our thinking along the way. Hermann Simon, a cofounder of the firm and a prolific author, reviewed our content and provided fundamental feedback. Shikha Jain deserves our sincere thanks for her invaluable contributions to the firm's commitment to sustainability. She drove the core sustainability studies that formed the basis for this book. Thanks to Tobias Maria Guenter and David Vidal for inspiring us by sharing their thinking and their experience. A few other partners at our firm steered us to the examples given throughout the book and opened doors to their executive suites. Thanks to our fellow partners Onno Oldeman, Jos Eeland, Philipp Biermann, Thomas Haller, and Silvio Struebi. A special thanks goes out to Lotte Moefelt for her support with organization behind the scenes. We also thank Ezra Blocker for his help with proofreading the manuscript and Elana Duffy for feedback on initial drafts.

Many thanks to the executives and business leaders who allowed us to tell their stories in detail: Vincent Clerc of A.P. Moller–Maersk, Leonhard Birnbaum of E.ON, Henk S. de Jong of Versuni, Andrea Baldo of GANNI, Régis Koenig of Fnac Darty, Tim Brooks of LEGO, Jan-Marc Fergg of HSBC, and Jens Gamborg of Bang & Olufsen.

We extend our gratitude to Catherine Woods, our executive editor at MIT Press, for recognizing the potential in our initial manuscript and for her role in shaping it. This gratitude extends to the rest of the MIT Press team for transforming our ideas into a physical and digital book.

We thank our family members especially for their nonstop encouragement and understanding. This book would not have been possible without their support.

Notes

Chapter 1

1. See a brief overview in Colby Hopkins, "The History of Amazon and Its Rise to Success," *Michigan Journal of Economics*, May 1, 2023, https://sites.lsa.umich.edu/mje/2023/05/01/the-history-of-amazon-and-its-rise-to-success/.

2. Michael H. Martin, "The Next Big Thing: A Bookstore?," *Fortune*, December 9, 1996, https://fortune.com/1996/12/09/amazon-bookstore-next-big-thing/.

3. Martin, "The Next Big Thing."

4. Martin Guerrieria, "Revealed: The World's Most Valuable Brands of 2023," Kantar, June 14, 2023, https://www.kantar.com/inspiration/brands/revealed-the-worlds-most-valuable-brands-of-2023.

5. "The First Day of Prime Day Was the Single Largest Sales Day Ever on Amazon, Helping Make This the Biggest Prime Day Event Ever," Amazon, July 13, 2023, https://www.aboutamazon.com/news/retail/amazon-prime-day-2023-stats.

6. Market data as of September 29, 2023, from MarketWatch, https://www.marketwatch.com/investing/stock/amzn.

7. Hermann Simon, *True Profit: No Company Ever Went Broke Turning a Profit* (New York: Springer, 2020), 15–16.

8. Throughout the book, for the sake of brevity we refer to sustainable products and services as "sustainable solutions."

9. Ann-Marie Alcántara, "Schick Designs a Disposable Razor to Appeal to Environmentally Conscious Consumers," *Wall Street Journal*, April 13, 2022, https://www.wsj.com/articles/schick-designs-a-disposable-razor-to-appeal-to-environmentally-conscious-consumers-11649844001; emphasis added.

10. This quote is widely attributed to Mead but we have not found a source that confirms she said or wrote those exact words.

11. For a recent confirmatory study on the power of repetition and the illusory truth effect, please see Aumyo Hassan and Sarah J. Barber, "The Effects of Repetition Frequency on the Illusory Truth Effect," *Cognitive Research: Principles and Implications* 6, no. 1 (2021): 38, https://www.ncbi.nlm.nih.gov/pmc/articles/PMC8116821/.

12. Euromonitor International, *Seizing the Opportunity in Sustainability* (London: Euromonitor International, 2022), https://www.euromonitor.com/seizing-the-opportunity-in-sustainability/report.

13. Talal Rafi, "Why Sustainability Is Crucial for Corporate Strategy," World Economic Forum, June 9, 2022, https://www.weforum.org/agenda/2022/06/why-sustainability-is-crucial-for-corporate-strategy/.

14. See Andreas von der Gathen and Mark Billige, "The Demand Revolution: It's Time to Unleash Your Commercial Creativity," Simon-Kucher, May 3, 2021, https://www.simon-kucher.com/en/insights/demand-revolution-its-time-unleash-your-commercial-creativity-0.

15. Hermann Simon and Martin Fassnacht, *Price Management: Strategy, Analysis, Decision, Implementation* (Cham, Switzerland: Springer, 2019), 46–81.

16. "Four Megatrends Underlying Amazon: E-Commerce and More," VettaFi, July 21, 2022, https://www.nasdaq.com/articles/four-megatrends-underlying-amazon%3A-e-commerce-and-more.

17. Simon and Fassnacht, *Price Management*.

18. Paul Lienert and Nathan Gomes, "Ford Again Warns on EV Results, Withdraws 2023 Forecast," Reuters, October 27, 2023, https://www.reuters.com/business/autos-transportation/ford-withdraws-2023-forecast-warns-ev-results-2023-10-26/#:~:text=Ford%20lost%20an%20estimated%20%2436%2C000,EV%20in%20the%20second%20quarter; Nicholas Gordon, "Ford Projects Its EV Division Will Lose $3 Billion in 2023 after Losing $2 Billion Last Year: 'Startups Lose Money,'" *Fortune*, March 24, 2023, https://fortune.com/2023/03/24/ford-motors-projects-loss-electric-vehicles-tesla/; Keith Naughton, "Ford Slides after Pulling Profit Forecast on Strike Impact," *Bloomberg*, October 26, 2023, https://www.bloomberg.com/news/articles/2023-10-26/ford-misses-on-profit-pulls-2023-outlook-after-settling-strike?sref=0xJNnLv0.

19. Simon-Kucher, *Sustainability Study 2022* (Bonn, Germany: Simon-Kutcher & Partners, October 24, 2022), https://www.simon-kucher.com/en/who-we-are/newsroom/sustainability-study-2022.

20. Onno Oldeman, Jos Eeland, David Boer, and Roos Offerhaus, "Monetizing Sustainability with Albert Heijn," Simon-Kucher, July 16, 2023, https://www.simon-kucher.com/en/insights/monetizing-sustainability-albert-heijn.

21. Peter F. Drucker, *The Practice of Management* (New York: HarperCollins, 2006), loc. 668 of 6962, Kindle.

22. Theodore Levitt, *Marketing Myopia* (Boston: Harvard Business Review Press, 2008), 6–7; Theodore Levitt, "Marketing Myopia," *Harvard Business Review*, September–October 1975, reprinted online in *Harvard Business Review*, July–August 2004, https://hbr.org/2004/07/marketing-myopia.

23. Colin Bryar and Bill Carr, *Working Backwards: Insights, Stories, and Secrets from Inside Amazon* (New York: St. Martin's Press, 2021), xi.

24. Stuart L. Hart and Mark B. Milstein, "Global Sustainability and the Creative Destruction of Industries," *MIT Sloan Management Review*, October 15, 1999, https://sloanreview.mit.edu/article/global-sustainability-and-the-creative-destruction-of-industries/.

25. See Mark Billige and Andreas von der Gathen, "Commercial Creativity: How Will You Respond to the Demand Revolution?," Simon-Kucher, May 4, 2021, https://www.simon-kucher.com/en/node/4626.

26. Joseph A. Schumpeter, *Capitalism, Socialism and Democracy* (1942; reprint, London: Routledge, 1994), 82–83.

27. Farley quoted in Keith Naughton, "Ford's CEO Sees EVs Helping Carmaker Pare Its $3 Billion Ad Budget," *Bloomberg*, June 1, 2022, https://www.bloomberg.com/news/articles/2022-06-01/ford-ceo-sees-evs-helping-carmaker-pare-its-3-billion-ad-budget#xj4y7vzkg.

28. Akash Sriram and Hyunjoo Jin, "Elon Musk's Embrace of Advertising at Tesla Grabs Marketers' Attention," Reuters, May 18, 2023, https://www.reuters.com/business/autos-transportation/elon-musks-embrace-advertising-tesla-grabs-marketers-attention-2023-05-17/.

29. European Commission, "Screening of Websites for 'Greenwashing': Half of Green Claims Lack Evidence," press release, January 28, 2021, https://ec.europa.eu/commission/presscorner/detail/en/ip_21_269.

30. Maxine Joselow, "'Greenhushing': Why Some Companies Quietly Hide Their Climate Pledges," *Washington Post*, July 13, 2023, https://www.washing tonpost.com/climate-environment/2023/07/13/greenhushing-climate-trend -corporations/.

31. Tim Brooks, vice president and global head of sustainability, LEGO Group, Simon-Kucher interview, October 12, 2023.

Chapter 2

1. Report quoted in "Consumers Demand Sustainable Products and Shopping Formats," *Forbes*, March 11, 2022, https://www.forbes.com/sites/gregpetro/2022 /03/11/consumers-demand-sustainable-products-and-shopping-formats/?sh =65e05d466a06.

2. See Clayton M. Christensen, Michael E. Raynor, and Rory McDonald, "What Is Disruptive Innovation?," *Harvard Business Review*, December 2015, https:// hbr.org/2015/12/what-is-disruptive-innovation.

3. "$1 Trillion Green Investment Matches Fossil Fuels for First Time," *Bloomberg*, January 26, 2023, https://www.bloomberg.com/news/articles/2023-01-26 /global-clean-energy-investments-match-fossil-fuel-for-first-time#xj4y7vzkg.

4. Jan-Marc Fergg, global head of ESG and managed solutions, HSBC, Simon-Kucher interview, June 5, 2023.

5. We define a transformative megatrend as one whose effects evolve and endure over decades and change lives on a global scale. Such megatrends include mass production, electrification, digitalization, and globalization.

6. Agnes Walton and Kristopher Knight, "New Climate Promises, Same Old Global Warming," *New York Times*, July 12, 2022, https://www.nytimes.com /video/opinion/100000008429698/net-zero-global-warming.html?campaign _id=39&emc=edit_ty_20220712&instance_id=66418&nl=opinion-today&regi _id=88108691&segment_id=98270&te=1&user_id=330004b32a47746792b827 b9f014dd37; Chris Mooney and Harry Stevens, "The U.S. Plan to Avoid Extreme Climate Change Is Running out of Time," *Washington Post*, July 18, 2022, https:// www.washingtonpost.com/climate-environment/2022/07/18/climate-change -manchin-math/?utm_campaign=wp_post_most&utm_medium=email&utm _source=newsletter&wpisrc=nl_most&carta-url=https://s2.washingtonpost.com /car-ln-tr/3768503/62d58160cfe8a21601f559b0/5c768fb5ade4e238493c43f9/8 /72/62d58160cfe8a21601f559b0&wp_cu=feb0117480ed582ad6220e46e502f510 %7C82E0D12842FE4D1DE0530100007FED03.

7. "Factual Food Labels: A Closer Look at the History," *Nutritional Science News and Highlights* (Department of Nutritional Sciences, University of Texas at Austin), April 6, 2018, https://he.utexas.edu/ntr-news-list/food-labels-history #:~:text=In%201990%2C%20the%20USDA%20mandated,products%20 intended%20to%20be%20sold.

8. United Nations Climate Action, "For a Livable Climate: Net-Zero Commitments Must Be Backed by Credible Action," accessed December 11, 2023, https://www.un.org/en/climatechange/net-zero-coalition.

9. María Coronado Robles, "From Sustainability to Purpose Q&A: Awareness, Communication and Investment," Euromonitor International, January 1, 2021, https://www.euromonitor.com/article/from-sustainability-to-purpose-qa -awareness-communication-and-investment.

10. Elisa Farri, Paolo Cervini, and Gabriele Rosani, "How Sustainability Efforts Fall Apart," *Harvard Business Review*, September 26, 2022, https://hbr.org/2022 /09/how-sustainability-efforts-fall-apart.

Chapter 3

1. Jem Aswad, "Coldplay's 'Music of the Spheres' Tour Drastically Reduces Band's Carbon Footprint, Sets New Standards in Sustainability," *Variety*, June 5, 2023, https://variety.com/2023/music/news/coldplay-tour-carbon-footprint -sustainability-green-1235632704/.

2. Vincent Clerc, CEO, A.P. Moller–Maersk, Simon-Kucher interview, August 16, 2023.

3. John Naisbitt and Patricia Aburdene, *Megatrends 2000: Ten New Directions for the 1990's* (New York: William Morrow, 1990), 12.

4. Virginia Hoekenga, "Andrew Winston: Gigatrends Shaping the Future," NAEM, October 7, 2020, https://www.naem.org/connect/blog/read/green-tie /2020/10/07/andrew-winston-gigatrends-shaping-future-business-planet. See also Daniel C. Esty and Andrew S. Winston, *Green to Gold: How Smart Companies Use Environmental Strategy to Innovate, Create Value, and Build Competitive Advantage* (Hoboken, NJ: Wiley, 2006); and Andrew S. Winston, *The Big Pivot: Radically Practical Strategies for a Hotter, Scarcer, and More Open World* (Boston: Harvard Business Review Press, 2014).

5. Hajkowicz quoted in Anna Anetta Janowska and Radosław Malik, "Megatrends and Their Use in Economic Analyses of Contemporary Challenges in

the World Economy," *Prace Naukowe Uniwersytetu Ekonomicznego we Wrocławiu*, January 2018, https://doi.org/10.15611/pn.2018.523.18.

6. Jobs quoted in Walter Isaacson, *Steve Jobs* (New York: Simon & Schuster, 2013), loc. 8960 of 11659, Kindle.

7. "UN / GUTERRES IPCC REPORT," March 20, 2023, UN Audiovisual Library, https://www.unmultimedia.org/avlibrary/asset/3022/3022200/#:~:text=UN%20Secretary%2DGeneral%20Ant%C3%B3nio%20Guterres%20said%20that%20the%20new%20IPCC,on%20all%20fronts%20%2D%2D%20everything%2C.

8. Justin McGuirk, "The Waste Age," Aeon, accessed December 13, 2023, https://aeon.co/essays/ours-is-the-waste-age-thats-the-key-to-tranforming-the-future.

9. "*Silent Spring*, Rachel Carson, 1962," description of archived book at the Smithsonian Institution, accessed December 13, 2023, https://www.si.edu/object/silent-spring-rachel-carson-1962%3Anmah_1453548.

10. "A Short History of a Ground-Breaking Publication: *The Limits to Growth*," Club of Rome, February 2022, https://www.cluboforme.org/wp-content/uploads/2022/02/CoR-LtG-ShortHistory.pdf.

11. *Our Common Future: Report of the World Commission on Environment and Development* [Brundtland Commission] (United Nations, 1987), 41, https://sustainabledevelopment.un.org/content/documents/5987our-common-future.pdf.

12. Al Gore, *Earth in the Balance: Forging a New Common Purpose* (1992; New York: Routledge, 2007), loc. 77–78 and 6189 of 8585, Kindle.

Chapter 4

1. Tensie Whelan and Randi Kronthal-Sacco, "Actually, Consumers Do Buy Sustainable Products," Stern Center for Sustainable Business, New York University, June 19, 2019, https://www.stern.nyu.edu/experience-stern/faculty-research/actually-consumers-do-buy-sustainable-products.

2. Florian Heineke, Nadine Janecke, Holger Klärner, Florian Kühn, Humayun Tai, and Raffael Winter, "Renewable-Energy Development in a Net-Zero World," McKinsey & Company Electric Power & Natural Gas Practice, October 28, 2022, https://www.mckinsey.com/industries/electric-power-and-natural-gas/our-insights/renewable-energy-development-in-a-net-zero-world.

3. "The Energy Transition Will Be Volatile," *Energy Source, Financial Times,* June 2023, https://www.ft.com/content/86d71297-3f34-48f3-8f3f-28b7e8be03c6.

4. Boston Consulting Group, "The Electric Car Tipping Point," 2018, https://web-assets.bcg.com/ef/8b/007df7ab420dab1164e89d0a6584/bcg-the-electric-car-tipping-point-jan-2018.pdf; Boston Consulting Group, "Electric Cars Are Finding Their Next Gear," 2022, https://www.bcg.com/publications/2022/electric-cars-finding-next-gear; Boston Consulting Group, "Why Electric Cars Can't Come Fast Enough," 2021, https://www.bcg.com/publications/2021/why-evs-need-to-accelerate-their-market-penetration.

5. Recurrent Auto, "EV Adoption, Trends & Statistics in the US," 2022, https://www.recurrentauto.com/research/ev-adoption-us. The same applies to other companies that play a role in the automotive industry's ecosystem all along the value chain.

6. Our firm and the team that worked on this book also have extensive experience with identifying, unscrambling, and interpreting demand signals and turning them into concrete commercial strategies on value propositions, product design, pricing, communication, and go-to-market strategies.

7. Simon-Kucher, *Sustainability Study 2022* (Bonn, Germany: Simon-Kutcher & Partners, October 24, 2022), https://www.simon-kucher.com/en/who-we-are/newsroom/sustainability-study-2022.

8. Allied Market Reseearch, "Luxury Apparel Market Value Worldwide from 2020 to 2031," Statista, 2022, https://www.statista.com/statistics/941156/luxury-apparels-market-value-worldwide/; Research and Markets, "Fast Fashion Market Value Forecast Worldwide from 2021 to 2026," Statista, 2022, https://www.statista.com/statistics/1008241/fast-fashion-market-value-forecast-worldwide/.

9. Henk de Jong, CEO, Versuni, Simon-Kucher interview, March 22, 2023.

10. thredUP, "Secondhand Apparel Market Value Worldwide," Statista, 2022, https://www.statista.com/statistics/1008524/secondhand-apparel-market-value-by-segment-worldwide/.

11. Andrea Baldo, CEO, GANNI, Simon-Kucher interview, March 20, 2023; unless otherwise noted, quotes from Baldo in this chapter come from this interview.

12. World Economic Forum, "The World Needs a Circular Economy: Help Us Make It Happen," January 22, 2020, https://www.weforum.org/agenda/2020/01/the-world-needs-a-circular-economy-lets-make-it-happen/; Earth Overshoot Day, 2023, https://www.overshootday.org/.

13. Onno Oldeman, Jos Eeland, David Boer, and Roos Offerhaus, "Monetizing Sustainability with HEMA," Simon-Kucher, July 24, 2023, https://www.simon -kucher.com/en/insights/monetizing-sustainability-hema.

14. For more information on these companies, see Marco Bertini and Oded Koenigsberg, *The Ends Game: How Smart Companies Stop Selling Products and Start Delivering Value* (Cambridge, MA: MIT Press, 2022).

15. Our World in Data, "Global Greenhouse Gas Emissions by Sector," 2020, https://ourworldindata.org/emissions-by-sector.

16. Statista, *Shared Mobility Report 2022* (2022), 17, https://www.statista.com /study/40459/mobility-services-report/; Statista, "Revenue of Passenger Cars Worldwide," 2022, https://www.statista.com/outlook/mmo/passenger-cars/world wide#revenue.

17. Airbnb, "Revenue of Airbnb Worldwide from 2017–2022," Statista, 2022, https://www.statista.com/statistics/1193134/airbnb-revenue-worldwide/.

18. eMarketer, "Direct-to-Consumer (D2C) E-commerce Sales in the United States from 2019 to 2024," Statista, 2022, https://www.statista.com/statistics /1109833/usa-d2c-ecommerce-sales/.

19. Organization for Economic Cooperation and Development (OECD), fore- word to *Globalisation, Comparative Advantage and the Changing Dynamics of Trade* (Paris: OECD, 2011), https://www.oecd.org/publications/globalisation -comparative-advantage-and-the-changing-dynamics-of-trade-9789264113084 -en.htm.

20. Ethical Consumer, *Ethical Consumerism Report 2021: Can We Consume Back Better?* (Manchester, UK: Ethical Consumer, 2021), https://research.ethicalcon sumer.org/sites/default/files/inline-files/EC_Market_Report_2021.pdf; UK Office for National Statistics, "Turnover of Retail Trade (except of Motor Vehicles and Motor-cycles) in the United Kingdom (UK) from 2008 to 2020," Statista, 2023, https://www.statista.com/statistics/309108/retail-turnover-united-kingdom-uk/.

21. Onno Oldeman, Jos Eeland, David Boer, and Roos Offerhaus, "Monetizing Sustainability with Albert Heijn," Simon-Kucher, July 16, 2023, https://www .simon-kucher.com/en/insights/monetizing-sustainability-albert-heijn.

22. Allied Market Research, "Natural and Organic Cosmetics and Personal Care," Statista, 2022, https://www.statista.com/statistics/673641/global-market -value-for-natural-cosmetics/; Statista, "Beauty and Personal Care," 2023, https:// www.statista.com/outlook/cmo/beauty-personal-care/worldwide.

23. Hannah Ritchie, "Food Production Is Responsible for One-Quarter of the World's Greenhouse Gas Emissions," Our World in Data, November 6, 2019, https://ourworldindata.org/food-ghg-emissions; Statista, "Food: United States," 2023, https://www.statista.com/outlook/cmo/food/united-states#revenue; US Organic Trade Association, *Organic Industry Survey 2022* (Washington, DC: US Organic Trade Association, 2022), https://ota.com/market-analysis/organic-industry-survey/organic-industry-survey.

24. Unilever, "Unilever Reveals Influencers Can Switch People On to Sustainable Living," March 9, 2023, https://www.unilever.com/news/press-and-media/press-releases/2023/unilever-reveals-influencers-can-switch-people-on-to-sustainable-living/.

25. Alon Ghelber, "Customer Experience Is Key as Consumers Share More Online Reviews," *Forbes*, August 3, 2021, https://www.forbes.com/sites/forbescommunicationscouncil/2021/08/03/customer-experience-is-key-as-consumers-share-more-online-reviews/?sh=7dda7f75362c.

26. US Environmental Protection Agency, "Containers and Packaging: Product-Specific Data," 2018, https://www.epa.gov/facts-and-figures-about-materials-waste-and-recycling/containers-and-packaging-product-specific.

27. DS Smith, "DS Smith Survey Reveals Pandemic Embrace of Recycling and Sustainability," 2021, https://www.dssmith.com/us/media/newsroom2/2021/10/ds-smith-survey-pandemic-shopping/.

28. Onno Oldeman, Jos Eeland, David Boer, and Roos Offerhaus, "Monetizing Sustainability with C&A," Simon-Kucher, August 1, 2023, https://www.simon-kucher.com/en/insights/monetizing-sustainability-ca.

29. David Feber, Anna Granskog, Oskar Lingqvist, and Daniel Nordigård, "Sustainability in Packaging: Inside the Minds of US Consumers," McKinsey & Company, October 21, 2020, https://www.mckinsey.com/industries/paper-forest-products-and-packaging/our-insights/sustainability-in-packaging-inside-the-minds-of-us-consumers.

30. US Department of Agriculture, "Food Loss and Waste," accessed December 13, 2023, https://www.usda.gov/foodlossandwaste.

31. Grand View Research, "Size of the Meal Kit Service Market Worldwide from 2021 to 2030," Statista, 2022, https://www.statista.com/statistics/655037/global-direct-to-door-meal-kit-service-market-revenue/.

Chapter 5

1. "The Half-Truth of First-Mover Advantage," *Harvard Business Review*, April 2005, https://hbr.org/2005/04/the-half-truth-of-first-mover-advantage.

2. P. N. Golder and G. J. Tellis, "Pioneer Advantage: Marketing Logic or Marketing Legend?," *Journal of Marketing Research* 30, no. 2 (May 1993): 167.

3. Ipsos, *Global Trends 2020* (Paris: Ipsos, 2020), 42, https://www.ipsos.com/sites/default/files/ct/publication/documents/2020-02/ipsos-global-trends-2020-understanding-complexity.pdf.

4. Andrea Baldo, CEO, GANNI, Simon-Kucher interview, March 20, 2023; Henk de Jong, CEO, Versuni, Simon-Kucher interview, March 22, 2023.

5. "The Half-Truth of First-Mover Advantage."

6. Simon-Kucher, *Sustainability Study 2022* (Bonn, Germany: Simon-Kucher & Partners, October 24, 2022), https://www.simon-kucher.com/en/who-we-are/newsroom/sustainability-study-2022.

7. GlobalData, *TrendSights Analysis 2022: Sustainability and Ethics* (London: GlobalData, 2022), https://www.globaldata.com/store/report/sustainability-and-ethics-consumer-trend-analysis/.

8. "Empowered Consumers Call for Sustainability Transformation," *Forbes*, January 21, 2021, https://www.forbes.com/sites/forrester/2021/01/21/empowered-consumers-call-for-sustainability-transformation/?sh=88035bd2042f.

9. Leonhard Birnbaum, CEO, E.ON, Simon-Kucher interview, April 20, 2023; subsequent quotes from Birbaum in this chapter also come from this interview.

10. "The Energy Transition Will Be Volatile," *Financial Times,* June 2023, https://www.ft.com/content/86d71297-3f34-48f3-8f3f-28b7e8be03c6.

Chapter 6

1. Simon-Kucher, *Sustainability Study 2022* (Bonn, Germany: Simon-Kucher & Partners, October 24, 2022), https://www.simon-kucher.com/en/who-we-are/newsroom/sustainability-study-2022.

2. The product categories were as follows, with examples in parentheses: grocery and household shopping (food and nonfood), apparel/fashion/footwear, beauty and personal care, electronics and household appliances, furniture,

restaurants, mobility via own means (cars, motorcycles), on-demand private mobility (taxis, ride sharing, e-scooter), local public transportation (buses, trains, trams), long-distance transportation (trains, planes, coaches), places to stay (hotels, hostels, holiday rental homes), holiday/vacation packages (package holiday rental homes), heating (usage, fuel sources), electricity, personal financial investments (mutual funds/exchange-traded funds, stocks, retirement funds), cryptocurrencies (Bitcoin, blockchain, other decentralized currencies), personal banking (checking account, current account, savings account), personal borrowing (mortgages, asset finance, credit cards, and personal loans), and home construction/renovation (e.g., products such as paints and coatings, windows and wallboards, tiles and flooring, plumbing and heating).

3. Geoffrey A. Moore, *Crossing the Chasm: Marketing and Selling Disruptive Products to Mainstream Consumers*, 3rd ed. (New York: Harper Business, 2014), loc. 349 of 4233, Kindle.

Chapter 8

1. The conversation with Jennifer took place in early June 2023, the week that New York registered the worst recorded air quality in the city's history. For more information, see Aatish Bhatia, Josh Katz, and Margot Sanger-Katz, "Just How Bad Was the Pollution in New York?," *New York Times*, June 8, 2023, https://www.nytimes.com/interactive/2023/06/08/upshot/new-york-city-smoke.html.

2. The calculation of operating costs for EVs and fuel-powered vehicles is much different in the United States and Europe because in Europe fuel costs per gallon tend to be much higher. This may make the perceived savings in Europe greater than in the United States, all else being equal.

3. For TOMS's claims regarding its sustainability, see its website at https://www.toms.com/us/impact/planet.html.

4. For Rothy's claims regarding its sustainability, see its website at https://rothys.com/pages/sustainability.

Chapter 10

1. Maersk, *2022 Sustainability Report* (Copenhagen, Denmark: Maersk, 2022), maersk.com/sustainability/reports-and-resources.

2. Leonhard Birnbaum, CEO, E.ON, Simon-Kucher interview, April 20, 2023.

3. Al Ries and Jack Trout, *Positioning: The Battle for Your Mind* (New York: McGraw Hill, 2001), 19.

4. Schumacher quoted in Niamh Carroll, "Unilever CEO: We Will Stop 'Force Fitting' Purpose to Our Brands," *MarketingWeek*, October 26, 2023, https://www.marketingweek.com/unilever-ceo-stop-force-fitting-purpose-brands/.

5. Ries and Trout, *Positioning*, 24–25.

6. Tim Brooks, vice president and global head of sustainability, LEGO Group, Simon-Kucher interview, September 8, 2023; all quotations from Brooks in this chapter come from this interview.

7. See GlobalData, *TrendSights Analysis 2022: Sustainability and Ethics* (London: GlobalData, 2022), https://www.globaldata.com/store/report/sustainability-and-ethics-consumer-trend-analysis/; and Capgemini Research Institute, *How Sustainability Is Fundamentally Changing Consumer Preferences* (Paris: Capgemeni Research Institute, 2020).

Chapter 11

1. "Ford, SK On [*sic*] Make Significant Construction Progress at Blueoval SK Battery Park, On-Plan to Train 5,000 Employees at On-Site Training Center," Ford Newsroom, December 12, 2022, https://media.ford.com/content/fordmedia/fna/us/en/news/2022/12/05/ford--sk-on-make-significant-construction-progress-at-blueoval-s.html.

2. Joseph White, Paul Lienert, and Nathan Gomes, "Ford Slows EV Ramp as Second-Quarter Commercial-Vehicle Profit Booms," Reuters, July 27, 2023, https://www.reuters.com/business/autos-transportation/ford-raises-annual-pre-tax-profit-view-supply-chain-woes-ease-2023-07-27/; Paul Lienert and Nathan Gomes, "Ford Again Warns on EV Results, Withdraws 2023 Forecast," Reuters, October 26, 2023, https://www.reuters.com/business/autos-transportation/ford-withdraws-2023-forecast-warns-ev-results-2023-10-26/.

3. Dan Neil, "2022 Ford F-150 Lightning: The Everyman's EV," *Wall Street Journal*, May 12, 2022, https://www.wsj.com/articles/2022-ford-f-150-lightning-review-11652388946.

4. "Ford Opens Cologne EV Center—Home of a New Generation of Electric Vehicles—First Carbon Neutral Assembly Plant," Ford Newsroom, June 12, 2023, https://media.ford.com/content/fordmedia/fna/us/en/news/2023/06/12/ford

-opens-cologne-ev-center.html#:~:text=The%20Cologne%20EV%20Center%20
will,and%20direct%20suppliers%20by%202035.

5. Bruce quoted in Harry Dempsey, Kana Inagaki, Christian Davies, and Song Jung-a, "How Solid State Batteries Could Transform Transport," *Financial Times*, October 27, 2023, https://www.ft.com/content/f4353d2b-f941-475b-bc1d-a644 75503ea6.

6. Jeffrey Pfeffer and Robert I. Sutton, *The Knowing–Doing Gap: How Smart Companies Turn Knowledge into Action* (Boston: Harvard Business Review Press, 2000), loc. 518–519 of 4392, Kindle.

7. Madhavan Ramanujam and Georg Tacke, *Monetizing Innovation: How Smart Companies Design the Product around the Price* (Hoboken, NJ: Wiley, 2016), 8.

8. Keith Flamer, updated by Justin Krajeski, "Do Laundry Detergent Sheets Work as Well as Liquid?," *Consumer Reports*, updated October 23, 2023, https://www.consumerreports.org/appliances/laundry-detergents/laundry-detergent -sheets-review-a8916087070/.

9. US Environmental Protection Agency, "Plastics: Material-Specific Data," accessed December 14, 2023, https://www.epa.gov/facts-and-figures-about-ma terials-waste-and-recycling/plastics-material-specific-data.

10. Unilever, "Unilever Brings Innovation to Laundry Sheets in Mass Market First," July 26, 2023, https://www.unilever.com/news/news-search/2023/unilever -brings-innovation-to-laundry-sheets-in-mass-market-first/.

11. Jodhaira Rodriguez, "5 Best Laundry Detergent Sheets, Tested by Cleaning Experts," *Good Housekeeping*, updated October 30, 2023, https://www.good housekeeping.com/home-products/laundry-detergents/g41423872/best-laundry -detergent-sheets/.

12. Flamer, "Do Laundry Detergent Sheets Work as Well as Liquid?"

13. Luis Gomez, "Why Industry Collaboration Is Necessary for a Sustainable Future," World Economic Forum, March 17, 2023, https://www.weforum.org /agenda/2023/03/radical-collaboration-for-a-sustainable-future-the-case-for -sustainability-collaboration/.

14. Hyunjoo Jin, David Shepardson, and Abhirup Roy, "Ford Strikes Deal with Tesla to Gain Access to Rival Charging Stations Starting 2024," Reuters, May 25, 2023, https://www.reuters.com/business/autos-transportation/tesla-ford-ceos-talk -evs-twitter-forum-2023-05-25/.

15. *Consumer Reports* survey cited in Greg Norman, "Electric Car Survey Finds This as the Biggest Reason Preventing People from Buying Them," FoxBusiness, July 11, 2022, https://www.foxbusiness.com/economy/electric-car-survey-finds -biggest-reason-preventing-people-buying.

16. Hannah Lutz, "EV Inventory Reaches Critical Mass in U.S., Cox Says," *Automotive News*, June 27, 2023, https://www.autonews.com/retail/why-ev-inventories -are-rising-car-dealer-lots.

17. Cox Automotive, "New Cox Automotive Study: EV Consideration at Record High, but Dealers Feel Unprepared," press release, June 27, 2023, https://www .coxautoinc.com/news/new-cox-automotive-study-ev-consideration-at-record -high-but-dealers-feel-unprepared/; Lutz, "EV Inventory Reaches Critical Mass in U.S., Cox Says."

18. See Loop's website at https://exploreloop.com/.

19. Vincent Clerc, CEO, Maersk, Simon-Kucher interview, August 16, 2023.

20. See Mark Billige and Andreas von der Gathen, "Commercial Creativity: How Will You Respond to the Demand Revolution?," Simon-Kucher paper, May 4, 2021, https://www.simon-kucher.com/en/node/4626.

21. Jan-Marc Fergg, global head, ESG & Managed Solutions, HSBC, Simon-Kucher interview, June 5, 2023.

22. Joseph A. Schumpeter, *Capitalism, Socialism and Democracy* (1942; reprint, London: Routledge, 1994), 82–83.

23. Paige Hodder, "Internal Combustion Engine Suppliers Face Shakeout amid EV Transition, S&P Says," *Automotive News*, May 4, 2023, https://www.autonews .com/suppliers/ice-suppliers-face-shakeout-amid-ev-transition; Richard Truett, "How E-Fuel Could Extend the Life of ICE Vehicles in the Electric Age," *Automotive News*, July 7, 2023, https://www.autonews.com/mobility-report/how -carbon-neutral-e-fuels-could-extend-life-ice-vehicle.

24. IFPI, "IFPI Global Music Report: Global Recorded Music Revenues Grew 9% in 2022," March 21, 2023, https://www.ifpi.org/ifpi-global-music-report-global -recorded-music-revenues-grew-9-in-2022/.

Chapter 12

1. "Sales of Fax Machines in the United States from 1990 to 2010," table, Statista, accessed December 14, 2023, https://www.statista.com/statistics/191863/sales -of-fax-machines-in-the-us-since-2005/.

2. Andy Ash, "How Blockbuster Went from Dominating the Video Business to Bankruptcy," video and text, *Business Insider*, August 12, 2020, https://www .businessinsider.com/the-rise-and-fall-of-blockbuster-video-streaming-2020-1.

3. Netflix 10-K filing for fiscal year ending December 31, 2017, US Securities and Exchange Commission, https://www.sec.gov/Archives/edgar/data/1065280 /000106528018000069/q4nflx201710k.htm; Tom Huddleston, "Netflix Didn't Kill Blockbuster—How Netflix Almost Lost the Movie Rental Wars," CNBC, January 12, 2021, https://www.cnbc.com/2020/09/22/how-netflix-almost-lost -the-movie-rental-wars-to-blockbuster.html.

4. John Antioco, "How I Did It: Blockbuster's Former CEO on Sparring with an Activist Shareholder," *Harvard Business Review*, April 2011, https://hbr.org /2011/04/how-i-did-it-blockbusters-former-ceo-on-sparring-with-an-activist -shareholder.

5. Antioco, "How I Did It." See also Brett Hurt, "Lessons from a Blockbuster Failure," *Wharton Magazine*, February 17, 2014, https://magazine.wharton.upenn .edu/digital/lessons-from-a-blockbuster-failure/.

6. "Kodak's Digital Revenue Exceeds Film Sales in '05," *Los Angeles Times*, January 31, 2006, https://www.latimes.com/archives/la-xpm-2006-jan-31-fi-kodak31 -story.html.

7. Chunka Mui, "How Kodak Failed," *Forbes*, January 18, 2012, https://www .forbes.com/sites/chunkamui/2012/01/18/how-kodak-failed/?sh=55b66c346f27.

8. Burley quoted in Rupert Neate, "Kodak Falls in the 'Creative Destruction of the Digital Age,'" *The Guardian*, January 19, 2012, https://www.theguardian.com /business/2012/jan/19/kodak-bankruptcy-protection.

9. Willy Shih, "The Real Lessons from Kodak's Decline," *MIT Sloan Management Review*, May 20, 2016, https://sloanreview.mit.edu/article/the-real-lessons-from -kodaks-decline/.

10. Shigetaka Komori, *Innovating out of Crisis: How Fuji Film Survived (and Thrived) as Its Core Business Was Vanishing* (Berkeley, CA: Stone Bridge Press, 2015), loc. 116, 986, and 998 of 2057, Kindle.

11. Kodak 10-K filing for the year ending December 2022, US Securities and Exchange Commission, https://investor.kodak.com/node/20006/html#i1.

12. Fujifilm Holdings Corporation, *Earnings Presentation: Financial Results for FY 2022*, May 10, 2023, https://ir.fujifilm.com/en/investors/ir-materials/earnings

-presentations/main/01110/teaserItems5/00/linkList/0/link/ff_20233q4
_001.pdf.

13. Shih, "The Real Lessons from Kodak's Decline."

14. David Sheppard, "World at 'Beginning of End' of Fossil Fuel Era, Says Global Energy Agency," *Financial Times*, September 11, 2023, https://www.ft .com/content/9df6003b-3760-4eee-b189-92c0247fa1a5.

15. Andrew Edgecliffe-Johnson and Jamie Smyth, "Chevron's Mike Wirth: 'We Are Not Selling a Product That Is Evil,'" *Financial Times*, October 22, 2023, https://www.ft.com/content/1902a8ef-7078-47e2-8a62-b6f0050ed569?acce ssToken=zwAGCF6zBBCAkc8ZAqjvcHhH4tOKYrbwBQ7VaQ.MEYCIQCmw 21phJ4_K7qfiR0kAen4TLE1Itq8US28dPbdJS5GowIhAPLsLnxt7wYXrRxeiKS 0Kobi4qUXmk662jo96Urtm8xP&sharetype=gift&token=9d8bf7fa-21de-4d81 -84cf-d1a13759209b.

16. "Chevron Bets on Peak Green Energy," editorial, *Wall Street Journal*, October 23, 2023, https://www.wsj.com/articles/chevron-bets-on-peak-green-energy -99e72109?mod=opinion_lead_pos1.

17. Samantha Subin, "Tesla Hits $1 Trillion Market Cap for the First Time after Hertz Says It Will Buy 100,000 Electric Vehicles," CNBC, October 25, 2021, https://www.cnbc.com/2021/10/25/tesla-shares-up-on-news-hertz-will-purchase -100000-electric-vehicles.html.

18. Gates quoted in Catherine Clifford, "Bill Gates Says Climate Tech Will Produce 8 to 10 Teslas, a Google, an Amazon and a Microsoft," CNBC, October 20, 2021, https://www.cnbc.com/2021/10/20/bill-gates-expects-8-to-10-teslas-and-a -google-amazon-and-microsoft.html.

19. Fink quoted in Catherine Clifford, "Blackrock CEO Larry Fink: The Next 1,000 Billion-Dollar Start-Ups Will Be in Climate Tech," CNBC, October 25, 2021, https://www.cnbc.com/2021/10/25/blackrock-ceo-larry-fink-next-1000 -unicorns-will-be-in-climate-tech.html.

20. Colin Bryar and Bill Carr, *Working Backwards: Insights, Stories, and Secrets from Inside Amazon* (New York: St. Martin's Press, 2021), 98.

21. Peter Holderith, "With 120 Pumps This BUC-EE's Is Even Bigger Than the Rest with 350 Employees Required to Keep It Running 24/7," *The Drive*, June 29, 2023, https://www.thedrive.com/news/worlds-largest-gas-station-is-a -new-buc-ees-with-120-pumps; BUC-EE's, "World Records: The World's Largest

Convenience Store," accessed December 14, 2023, https://buc-ees.com/about /world-record-holder/.

22. Tesla provides information (including a map) online about where its charging stations are; for example, the one at the BUC-EE's in New Braunfels, Texas, is shown at https://www.tesla.com/findus/location/supercharger/New BraunfelsTXSupercharger.

23. See the Toyota Woven City website at https://www.woven-city.global.

24. For more on Neom, see https://www.neom.com/en-us/about.

25. Federal Office of Transport, Confédération suisse, "Underground Freight Transport," accessed December 14, 2023, https://www.bav.admin.ch/bav/en /home/modes-of-transport/cargo-sous-terrain.html.

26. Mark Tutton, "Self-Driving Pods Could Transport Frieght in Tunnels beneath Switzerland," CNN Travel, August 7, 2023, https://www.cnn.com/2023 /08/07/travel/self-driving-underground-pods-switzerland-cargo-sous-terrain /index.html.

Chapter 13

1. Renske van den Berge, Lise Magnier, and Ruth Mugge, "Too Good to Go? Consumers' Replacement Behaviour and Potential Strategies for Stimulating Product Retention," *Current Opinion in Psychology* 39 (June 2021): 66, https:// www.sciencedirect.com/science/article/pii/S2352250X20301226.

2. Fnac Darty, "Sustainable Consumption," accessed December 14, 2023, https:// www.fnacdarty.com/en/esg-commitments/sustainable-consumption/; Fnac Darty, "Fnac Darty Anounces Its New Strategic Plan, Everyday, Which Revolution- izes the Place of Advice, Sustainability and Service at the Heart of Day-to-Day Work for All Customers," February 23, 2021, https://www.fnacdarty.com/wp -content/uploads/2021/02/CP_Fnac-Darty-Everyday_vDEF_ENG-2.pdf.

3. Régis Koenig, director, Repair Operations & Durability, Fnac Darty, Simon- Kucher interview, October 12, 2023; all quotations from Koenig in this chapter come from this interview.

4. Fnac Darty subscription service prices accessed at https://www.darty.com /achat/services/darty-max/index.html, December 15, 2023.

5. Fnac Darty, "Fnac Darty Anounces Its New Strategic Plan, Everyday."

6. Fnac Darty, "2022 Annual Results," February 23, 2023, https://www.fnacdarty
.com/en/resultats-annuels-2022/; Fnac Darty, "Continued Implementation of
the Strategic Plan Everyday," October 26, 2023, https://www.fnacdarty.com/wp
-content/uploads/2023/10/fnac-darty-pr-q3-2023-26102023-vdef.pdf.

7. Ariat describes its sustainability practices at https://www.ariat.com/sustain
ability.

8. Jennie Bell, "Ariat Has Launched Its Own Secondhand Marketplace in Partnership with Archive," *Footwear News*, March 14, 2023, https://footwearnews
.com/business/business-news/ariat-launches-resale-marketplace-western-boots
-1203428239/.

9. For the Ariat Reboot offer, see https://reboot.ariat.com.

10. Andrea Baldo, CEO, GANNI, Simon-Kucher interview, March 20, 2023.

11. Yvon Chouinard, "Earth Is Now Our Only Shareholder," Patagonia,
accessed December 11, 2023, https://www.patagonia.com/ownership/.

12. Tamara Warren, "How Volvo Plans to Maintain Its Safety Rep While Stay-
ing in the Fast Lane," *TechCrunch*, December 11, 2021, https://techcrunch.com
/2021/12/11/how-volvo-plans-to-maintain-its-safety-rep-while-staying-in-the
-fast-lane/.

13. Julie Liesse, "How Purpose Tracks with Brand Purpose," in *Brand Purpose*
(Ad Age Datacenter, September 20, 2021), 6, https://go.na.kantar.com/brand
-purpose-report-pdf.

14. See TOMS's description of its sustainability practices at "About TOMS,"
https://www.toms.com/us/impact.html.

Chapter 14

1. Theodore Levitt, "Marketing Myopia," *Harvard Business Review*, September–
October 1975, reprinted online in *Harvard Business Review*, July–August 2004,
https://hbr.org/2004/07/marketing-myopia.

2. Marco Bertini and Oded Koenigsberg, *The Ends Game: How Smart Companies Stop Selling Products and Start Delivering Value* (Cambridge, MA: MIT Press,
2022), 49–50, 64–65.

3. Elon Musk, "The Mission of Tesla," November 18, 2013, https://www.tesla
.com/blog/mission-tesla.

4. "Tesla Cuts Vehicle Prices in Europe to Boost Demand," *Business Insider*, April 14, 2023, https://markets.businessinsider.com/news/stocks/tesla-cuts-vehicle -prices-in-europe-to-boost-demand-1032232959; "Largest Companies by Market Cap," accessed December 11, 2023, https://companiesmarketcap.com/; Tesla, *Impact Report 2022: A Sustainable Future Is within Reach* (Austin, TX: Tesla, 2022), https://www.tesla.com/impact.

5. Tesla, "Investor Day: Master Plan 3," accessed December 15, 2023, https:// digitalassets.tesla.com/tesla-contents/image/upload/IR/Investor-Day-2023 -Keynote.

6. Elon Musk, "The Tesla Approach to Distributing and Servicing Cars," Tesla blog, October 22, 2012, https://www.tesla.com/blog/tesla-approach-distributing -and-servicing-cars.

7. "Multiport Vehicle DC Charging System with Variable Power Distribution," US Patent US20130057209A1, patent application publication, accessed December 15, 2023, https://patents.google.com/patent/US20130057209A1/en.

8. David Trainer, "Tesla: Nothing New to See Here," *Forbes*, January 27, 2022, https://www.forbes.com/sites/greatspeculations/2022/01/27/tesla-nothing-new -to-see-here/?sh=2bf9b23b18d2.

9. Hyunjoo Jin, Joseph White, and Akash Sriram, "Tesla Vows to Halve EV Production Costs, Musk Keeps Affordable Car Plan under Wraps," Reuters, March 2, 2023, https://www.reuters.com/business/autos-transportation/elon-musk-ex pected-outline-more-affordable-ev-new-tesla-master-plan-2023-03-01/; Abinaya V and Aditya Soni, "Tesla Cuts US Prices for Sixth Time This Year ahead of Quarterly Results," Reuters, April 19, 2023, https://www.reuters.com/business/autos -transportation/tesla-cuts-us-prices-ahead-earnings-report-2023-04-19/; Victoria Waldersee, "Tesla to Build 25,000-Euro Car in Germany," Reuters, November 6, 2023, https://www.reuters.com/business/autos-transportation/tesla-build-25000 -euro-car-german-plant-source-2023-11-06/.

10. Elon Musk quoted in Jin, White, and Sriram, "Tesla Vows to Halve EV Production Costs."

11. Clayton Christensen, "Disruptive Innovation," accessed December 11, 2013, https://claytonchristensen.com/key-concepts.

12. Tesla Team, "Introducing Tesla Insurance," August 28, 2019, https://www .tesla.com/blog/introducing-tesla-insurance.

13. Sodastream, "Together We Can Make a Difference," accessed December 13, 2023, https://sodastream.com/blogs/explore/fight-plastic.

14. Sodastream, "Together We Can Make a Difference."

15. J. B. MacKinnon, *The Day the World Stops Shopping: How Ending Consumerism Saves the Environment and Ourselves* (New York: Ecco, 2021); Jamie Waters, "Overconsumption and the Environment: Should We All Stop Shopping?," *The Guardian*, May 30, 2021, https://www.theguardian.com/lifeandstyle/2021/may/30/should-we-all-stop-shopping-how-to-end-overconsumption.

16. "Double Shot of Sustainability: Ford and McDonald's Collaborate to Convert Coffee Bean Skin into Car Parts," Ford Newsroom, December 4, 2019, https://media.ford.com/content/fordmedia/fna/us/en/news/2019/12/04/ford-mcdonalds-collaboration-convert-coffee-bean-waste-into-car-parts.html; Dennis Green, "Adidas Is Getting Serious about Making Sneakers from Ocean Waste," *Business Insider*, April 21, 2017, https://www.businessinsider.com/adidas-releases-new-parley-ocean-waste-plastic-shoes-2017-4; "Adidas X Parley: For the Oceans," accessed December 11, 2013, https://www.adidas.de/en/parley.

17. "The Danish Deposit & Return System for Recycling Drink Cans and Bottles," State of Green, October 13, 2022, https://stateofgreen.com/en/solutions/the-danish-deposit-return-system-for-recycling-drink-cans-and-bottles/.

18. Partrice J. Williams, "Madewell Will Give You Money for Your Old Jeans—Here's Everything You Need to Know," *Reviewed*, February 7, 2019, https://reviewed.usatoday.com/lifestyle/features/what-you-need-to-know-about-the-madewell-denim-recycling-program.

19. Too Good to Go, *2022 Impact Report* (2022), https://www.toogoodtogo.com/en-us/download/2022-impact-report.

Chapter 15

1. Sheetal [*sic*], Rimjim Tyagi, and Gursimranjit Singh, "Gamification and Customer Experience in Online Retail: A Qualitative Study Focusing on Ethical Perspective," *Asian Journal of Business Ethics*, preprint online publication, December 2, 2022, https://www.ncbi.nlm.nih.gov/pmc/articles/PMC9716125/.

2. Rügenwalder Mühle, "Nachhaltigkeit bei der Rügenwalder Mühle: Wie macht ihr das eigentlich?," accessed December 11, 2023, https://www.ruegenwalder.de/de/nachhaltigkeit; Rügenwalder Mühle, "Über Uns: Alles rund um die Rügenwalder Mühle," accessed December 11, 2023, https://www.ruegen

walder.de/de/ueber-uns. The company's full name is Rügenwalder Mühle Carl Müller GmbH & Co. KG.

3. Rügenwalder Mühle, "Nachhaltigkeit bei der Rügenwalder Mühle," our translation.

4. Toby Myers, "How to Reduce a Pineapple's Carbon Footprint by > 20%," *Toby's Substack*, April 28, 2023, https://tobymyers.substack.com/p/how-to-reduce-a -pineapples-carbon?r=a4h3d&utm_campaign=post&utm_medium=web.

5. Katherine White, David J. Hardisty, and Rishad Habib, "The Elusive Green Consumer: People Say They Want Sustainable Products, but They Don't Tend to Buy Them. Here's How to Change That," *Harvard Business Review*, July–August 2019, https://hbr.org/2019/07/the-elusive-green-consumer.

6. "How Much Water Does It Really Take to Grow Almonds?," August 6, 2017, in *PAESTA*, podcast, episode 43, submitted by Laura Guertin, https://www.paesta .psu.edu/podcast/how-much-water-does-it-really-take-grow-almonds-paesta -podcast-series-episode-43; David R. Baker, Brian K. Sullivan, and Josh Saul, "California's Dry Season Is Turning into a Permanent State of Being," *Bloomberg*, August 12, 2021, https://www.bloomberg.com/news/articles/2021-08-12 /california-drought-a-dry-season-is-turning-into-drought-era.

7. Danish Veterinary and Food Administration, "About the Animal Welfare Label," accessed February 14, 2024, https://bedre-dyrevelfaerd.dk/om-dyrevel faerdsmaerket.

8. LEGO, "About Us," accessed December 11, 2023, https://www.lego.com/en -us/aboutus/lego-group/the-lego-brand?locale=en-us.

9. Tim Brooks, vice president and global head of sustainability, LEGO Group, Simon-Kucher interview, September 8, 2023; all quotes from Brooks in this chapter come from this interview.

10. LEGO, "Sustainable Packaging," accessed December 11, 2023, https://www .lego.com/en-us/sustainability/environment/sustainable-packaging.

11. Bricklink, "About the Team," accessed December 11, 2023, https://www .bricklink.com/v3/about.page.

12. ABS (acrylonitrile butadiene styrene) is a polymer blend known for its colorfastness, luster, and durability. For more information on it, see BPF, "Acrylonitrile Butadiene Styrene (ABS) and Other Specialist Styrenics," accessed December 11, 2023, https://www.bpf.co.uk/plastipedia/polymers/ABS_and_Other_Specialist _Styrenics.aspx.

13. Richard Milne, "Lego Ditches Oil-Free Brick in Sustainability Setback," *Financial Times*, September 25, 2023, https://on.ft.com/3RusDH3.

14. Paul Sillers, "Flight Carbon Calculators and Offsets: How Do They Work and Can We Trust Them?," CNN Travel, November 14, 2022, https://edition.cnn .com/travel/article/flight-carbon-calculator-methodologies/index.html#:~:text =This%20is%20mirrored%20in%20a,was%201%2D3%25.%E2%80%9D; Air Transport Action Group, "Fact Sheet #11: Voluntary Carbon Offsetting," November 2020, https://aviationbenefits.org/media/167226/fact-sheet_11_vol untary-carbon-offsetting_3.pdf.

15. Richard Thaler, "Nudge, Not Sludge," *Science*, August 3, 2013, https://www .science.org/doi/10.1126/science.aau9241.

Epilogue

1. Gates quoted in Catherine Clifford, "Bill Gates Says Climate Tech Will Produce 8 to 10 Teslas, a Google, an Amazon and a Microsoft," CNBC, October 20, 2021, https://www.cnbc.com/2021/10/20/bill-gates-expects-8-to-10-teslas-and-a -google-amazon-and-microsoft.html.

2. Simon-Kucher, *Sustainability Study 2022* (Bonn, Germany: Simon-Kutcher & Partners, October 24, 2022), https://www.simon-kucher.com/en/who-we-are /newsroom/sustainability-study-2022.

3. US Office of Energy Efficiency and Renewable Energy, "The Private Sector Accounts for 89% of Announced American-Made Battery Investments," FOTW #1315, November 6, 2023, https://www.energy.gov/eere/vehicles/articles/fotw -1315-november-6-2023-private-sector-accounts-89-announced-american-made.

4. Andrew R. Chow, "How ChatGPT Managed to Grow Faster Than TikTok or Instagram," *Time*, February 8, 2023, https://time.com/6253615/chatgpt-fastest -growing/.

5. MIT's report referenced in Bernard Marr, "Green Intelligence: Why Data and AI Must Become More Sustainable," *Forbes*, March 22, 2023, https://www .forbes.com/sites/bernardmarr/2023/03/22/green-intelligence-why-data-and-ai -must-become-more-sustainable/?sh=1d069a3a7658.

6. Francesco Bova, Avi Goldfarb, and Roger Melko, "The Business Case for Quantum Computing," *MIT Sloan Management Review*, March 7, 2023, https:// sloanreview.mit.edu/article/the-business-case-for-quantum-computing/#:~:text

=Quantum%20economic%20advantage%3A%20This%20occurs,scaling%20
is%20quadratic%20or%20polynomial.

7. European Commission, Finance, "Corporate Sustainability Reporting," accessed December 15, 2023, https://finance.ec.europa.eu/capital-markets-union-and-fin ancial-markets/company-reporting-and-auditing/company-reporting/corporate -sustainability-reporting_en.

8. Sam Meredith, "Shell's Board of Directors Sued over Climate Strategy in a First-of-Its-Kind Lawsuit," CNBC, February 9, 2023, https://www.cnbc.com/2023 /02/09/oil-shell-board-of-directors-sued-by-investors-over-climate-strategy.html.

9. Andrew Ross Sorkin, Jason Karaian, Sarah Kessler, Stephen Gandel, Michael J. de la Merced, Lauren Hirsch, and Ephrat Livni, "Activist Investors Assemble," *New York Times*, January 24, 2022, https://www.nytimes.com/2022/01/24/busi ness/dealbook/activists-unilever-peloton-kohls.html.

10. Peter Herweck and Peter Weckesser, "Digitalization Is the Key That Can Unlock Net-Zero for Industry," World Economic Forum, May 21, 2022, https:// www.weforum.org/agenda/2022/05/digitalization-key-net-zero-schneiderelectric/.

11. Bova, Goldfarb, and Melko, "The Business Case for Quantum Computing."

12. Lawler quoted in Joseph White, Paul Lienert, and Nathan Gomes, "Ford Slows EV Ramp as Second-Quarter Commercial-Vehicle Profit Booms," Reuters, July 27, 2023, https://www.reuters.com/business/autos-transportation/ford-raises -annual-pre-tax-profit-view-supply-chain-woes-ease-2023-07-27/.

Index